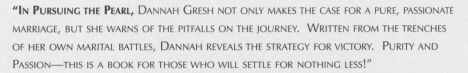
"IN PURSUING THE PEARL, DANNAH GRESH NOT ONLY MAKES THE CASE FOR A PURE, PASSIONATE MARRIAGE, BUT SHE WARNS OF THE PITFALLS ON THE JOURNEY. WRITTEN FROM THE TRENCHES OF HER OWN MARITAL BATTLES, DANNAH REVEALS THE STRATEGY FOR VICTORY. PURITY AND PASSION—THIS IS A BOOK FOR THOSE WHO WILL SETTLE FOR NOTHING LESS!"

— GARY D. CHAPMAN, PH.D. AUTHOR OF *THE FIVE LOVE LANGUAGES*

"IN THIS GEM OF A BOOK, DANNAH GRESH TAKES US ON THE TOPSY-TURVY JOURNEY WE CALL MARRIAGE. SHARING POIGNANT, PERSONAL STORIES, DANNAH MOVES US PAST THE HONEY-MOON TO THE STARK REALIZATION THAT THE JOURNEY IS OFTEN MARKED BY PAIN AND STRUGGLE AS WE FIND OURSELVES GROPING, TRIPPING AND FALLING ALONG THE WAY. THROUGH WELL-CRAFTED CHAPTERS AND SIMPLE EXERCISES DANNAH GUIDES US BACK TO THE LOVE WE ONCE KNEW—WHERE WE DISCOVER THAT THE JOURNEY IS INDEED WORTH IT. EACH AND EVERY STEP."

— DONNA VANLIERE, AUTHOR OF *THE CHRISTMAS SHOES* AND *THEY WALKED WITH HIM*

"THIS BOOK IS SORELY NEEDED IN THE BODY OF CHRIST. I SO MUCH APPRECIATE DANNAH AND BOB'S COURAGE IN BEING HONEST ABOUT THEIR PAINFUL STRUGGLES. THE CALL TO HOLINESS THAT DANNAH CHALLENGES US WITH IS, I BELIEVE, THE ANSWER TO DIVORCE IN THE BODY OF CHRIST. IT IS A WORK OF HUMILITY AND ENCOURAGEMENT FOR ALL CHRISTIAN COUPLES."

— ELIZABETH DUNCAN, *MARRIAGE AND FAMILY THERAPIST*

"I HAVE THE OPPORTUNITY TO TALK AND PRAY WITH HURTING AND CONFUSED CHRISTIAN MEN AND WOMEN WHOSE MARRIAGES ARE BEING PAINFULLY TORN APART. DANNAH'S BOOK IS AN INCREDIBLE SOURCE OF ENCOURAGEMENT AND HOPE TO PURSUE A PURE, PASSIONATE MARRIAGE."

— DEBBIE SIMMONS, WIFE, MOM, CHRISTIAN BOOKSTORE SALES ASSOCIATE

PURSUING

The Quest for a Pure, Passionate Marriage

THE PEARL

PURSUING

The Quest for a Pure, Passionate Marriage

THE PEARL

Dannah Gresh

Moody Press
CHICAGO

Library of Congress Cataloging-in-Publication Data
Gresh, Dannah.
      Pursuing the pearl : the quest for a pure, passionate marriage / Dannah Gresh.
      p. cm.
      ISBN 0-8024-8332-1
      1. Marriage. 2. Marriage–Religious aspects–Christianity. I.Title.

      HQ734 .G747 2002
      306.81–dc21

                                                                      2001055839

1 3 5 7 9 10 8 6 4 2
Printed in the United States of America

~ Contents ~

Fifteen years ago I met a girl named Dannah.

We fell in love, got engaged on stage in front of
two thousand people, and had a wonderful fairy
tale wedding. We were finally man and wife and
~~we lived happily ever after~~

~~we struggled a little, then~~ ~~lived happily ever after~~

we struggled and fought and laughed and cried and
questioned too many times whether we had made a
mistake by getting married at all.

Sometimes I wish my wife wrote about flowers or
animals. She could write a book on marketing or
Middle East politics and I'd be very happy. She
writes about none of these. She writes about
relationships and sex, and she doesn't write
fiction. And that's where the uneasiness sets in.
For before you finish this book, you will know more
about our marriage than I wish you to know. More
about our failures and intimate moments than my
pride wants to allow. Not that our marriage is
unique. That's just it. It's not.

God has a plan for this book. And a reason for you to read it. Before you finish this book, you will understand more about the perils of marriage—ours and yours—and you will recognize the hope and fulfillment that is available to you through God's love.

I hope you will read this book, identify with the heartache, remember the true love of your courtship, and use the information to do the hard work of pursuing God's best for your life and your marriage.

Some will not. The quest is both painful and risky. But if you choose to take it, you'll find the rich secrets to a pure and passionate marriage.

I say to you what I said to Dannah fifteen years ago:

- There is a Pearl of Great Price
- We are told to seek it
- We are commanded to purchase it
- It costs us everything
- It is worth the cost.

Come discover the secrets.

Bob

THE PEARL

"Again, the kingdom of heaven is like a merchant looking for fine pearls. When he found one of great value, he went away and sold everything he had and bought it."

MATTHEW 13:45–46

December 17, 1987
On Your Twentieth Birthday

My Dearest Dannah:

The last year has certainly been difficult—for both of us. However, even in the midst of those most difficult times, there is always a sense deep within, that we will not only survive but that we will prevail. We not only belong, we belong together. Over the past few weeks and months, I have come to understand that only after we begin to realize the joy that exudes from within our relationship, can we begin to realize the desperation of life without it.

- *There is a Pearl of Great Price.*
- *We are told to seek it.*
- *We are commanded to purchase it.*
- *It costs us everything.*
- *It is worth the cost!*

Purchase of the Pearl is only gained through a personal relationship with our Savior. However, there are many earthly parallels.

Dannah, you are my pearl of great price.
Your price is commitment.
Your love is worth the cost.

Bobby

I gently folded the tattered letter I'd treasured for the past seventeen months. I laid it beside the precious pearl earrings my groom had sent to me on this, our wedding day.

They were so simple and nondescript compared to the lavishly adorned costume pearl-drop earrings I'd planned to wear, but the choice was easy. I would relinquish these fake pearls and choose the simple round pearl studs. They were indescribably more valuable.

"[God's grace] teaches us to say 'No' to ungodliness

and worldly passions, and to live self-controlled,

upright and godly lives in this present age, while we

wait for the blessed hope—the glorious appearing of

our great God and Savior, Jesus Christ."

TITUS 2:12–13

CHAPTER ONE

Innocent Beginnings

Rrrrring. Rrrrrring.

I rolled over to ignore the phone, then realized where I was.

Rrrrring. Rrrrring.

I glanced toward the glass patio doors to be greeted by the breathtaking view from our honeymoon suite. The sun was just peaking over the clear blue ocean. The white-sand beach below me was being caressed by foamy waves. Birds flapped in the sun's morning rays.

Just a few weeks ago, the honeymoon plans weren't exactly meeting up to the fairy-tale wedding my parents were giving us. So, my crazy groom had conjured up a honeymoon "promotion." He'd promised to take me on my dream honeymoon as long as I was willing to (as the radio promos would say) share it with "a cast of thousands."

"Everyone loves romance," he'd assured me. "I can

get some hefty sponsors to pay for this thing if we just let the local radio audience, well . . . basically come with us!"

I didn't even give it a second thought. He got a local travel agency to buy the plane tickets, an upscale clothing store to kick in some advertising money, and Carnival Cruise Line's Crystal Palace in Nassau, Bahamas, to be the big sponsor. Everything was taken care of, from limo service to tickets for evening shows. All Bob and I had to do was cut some cheesy radio promos before the wedding and call back each day to keep people updated on everything we did . . . well, almost everything.

The radio audience loved it.

One day we had taken all of the listeners to visit the $25,000-a-night Galactica Suite at the top of the Crystal Palace. The room had a handprint entry pad that allowed authorized guests to enter. A robotic butler greeted guests, and the bedroom had three walls of two-story glass, placing the massive bed right out over the ocean. Of course, we had to go back to our little room. But, hey, it was a free little room with a view that didn't seem so modest before we'd been to the Galactica Suite!

I couldn't believe it was almost over. Tomorrow we would head home.

"Hello?" Bob croaked into the phone.

I glanced his way with a curious look on my face, wondering who would be calling.

"What!?" he said and cleared his voice quietly.

"It's John and the morning show," he mouthed to me.

"Well, we're just enjoying the beautiful morning sunrise," Bob said, trying to sound awake but failing miserably. It was obvious they were really giving him a hard time. I could imagine the fun they had with promos that morning. "We're gonna sneak right into Bob and Dannah's honeymoon suite this morning!"

Very funny! So, they wanted to heckle the honeymooners! I thought as I walked into the bathroom. I threw a little water on my face and swigged some mouthwash.

"Hey, Dannah," Bob shouted. "They want to talk to you! Your dad is in the studio!"

So, my dad is in on this, I thought. Well, two can play this little game.

My mind raced for some quick wit when suddenly something on the bathroom counter caught my eye.

"Tell them I can't come out of the bathroom right now," I requested. "You should probably warn them that there's already a new member of our family on the way!"

After an appropriate pregnant pause, I heard him convey the message. I could virtually see my father's face turning red!

I grabbed my inspiration from the countertop and rushed out to the phone.

"What's this about another family member?" John prodded with a hearty laugh. "Your dad is about to have heart failure."

"Hmmm?" I responded. "Maybe he shouldn't pick on honeymooners!"

John giggled.

"Last night we collected seashells to bring home with us," I reported.

"That's real romantic, Dannah," pushed John. "But aren't you changing the subject?"

"No," I answered innocently. "After I was so rudely awakened a few minutes ago, I found two of my seashells walking across the bathroom countertop!"

Laughter erupted in the radio studio, and a look of relief came over Bob's face as I opened my hand and showed him our new family members.

Minutes later we were wrapped in blankets and sitting on our balcony soaking in the view. The two tiny hermit crabs were on the table next to us scurrying around.

My husband wrapped his arms around me and pulled me closer. I could feel his rhythmic breathing as we sat there, speechless. No words were needed. No words could express how we felt.

I was sure this feeling would never end!

Everyone deserves to experience it . . . newlywed infatuation. That wonderful place where love is fueled not only by commitment but by *chemicals!* You have no trouble believing that a cheap apartment with a chipped vinyl-top table and mismatched chairs is the perfect spot for a romantic candlelight dinner. He only needs to touch your fingertips, and a rush of adrenaline ignites passion that erupts into sensuous butterflies in your stomach. You need only to glance knowingly at him, and he will drop *everything* to follow you *anywhere.* You are certain these feelings will never end.

But they do.

Sometimes it takes years. Sometimes it takes just a few weeks. But the chemical factory shuts down. And right behind the exit of the much-enjoyed adrenaline rush comes a dose of reality. You suddenly notice that strange, wheezy way he sneezes. He starts to wonder why you don't make chicken and noodles the way his mom did. You can't stand the way he "balances" his checkbook. He criticizes you for never trying to balance yours. It's not so funny anymore when he turns your favorite white pj's pink by washing them with the reds. He doesn't laugh anymore when you over-cook dinner.

What then? Just give up? Give in to the mundane, routine tolerance of marriage? Not me! No way! I wanted that "happily-ever-after" I'd always dreamed of living. I wanted a passionate and powerful love life.

I have a hunch that God wants the same thing for me. And for you. After all, He says in the Bible that the marriage relationship is meant to be a portrait of Christ's love for the church. Now that's a powerful, passionate, unending love!

But Satan has fueled an attack so great that within the church the divorce rates, stories of sexual immorality, and broken hearts rival the rest of the world's statistics. We end up misunderstanding the purpose of marriage and misusing the gift of sex without even knowing it. We find ourselves hopelessly distant in a relationship we'd hoped would be endlessly intimate.

Some try communication skills. Others turn to sexual technique manuals.

Some hire professionals. Others buy prescription antidepressants.

Some attend marriage seminars. Others buy an entire library of Christian marriage books.

I know. I've tried everything, too. But not one single good thing fit *into* my marriage until I took the time to aggressively get the junk *out* of my marriage! All the marriage books, communication skills, and sexual techniques in the world would not fix my marriage until I first learned to pursue purity.

Purity?! If you're like me, you breathed a big sigh of relief at the marriage altar because your journey for purity was over! But perhaps you've been married long enough to figure out that the journey is far from over. In my own marriage I've found that the struggle to have a pure heart that pursues

Christ at any cost is a daily battle. Every day I must choose to pursue my sweet Pearl of Great Price or to invest in and cling to this world's counterfeit offers.

Fake pearls of pride.

Fake pearls of social acceptance.

Fake pearls of social status.

Fake pearls of success.

These things have made my marriage really tough, and I'd like to tell you some of my story. I'm going to tell you some fun, romantic, and loving stories that my husband and I have written into our love life these past twelve years. And I'm going to take you to the depths of my rawest moments of pain.

Where Do We Begin?

It all starts with Titus 2:12–13. Those verses say that God's grace does not automatically keep us from worldly passions . . . what I would call fake pearls. Despite all of your love for God, your marriage could be blindsided . . . or maybe has been . . . by worldly passions. Worldly passions might include sexual temptation or tremendous moral failure, but that's just the obvious stuff. I want you to look more deeply into your own marriage to carefully identify any counterfeit pearls you might be investing in. Those might include greed for stuff, including a home it takes two incomes to keep or clothes and cars that run up the debt. They might include the pursuit of a title that costs many, many hours away from your family. It might include a struggle for power . . . or bitterness because you've lost the struggle. It might include putting your husband down as a form of humor that makes you the life of the party.

It doesn't take much for worldly passions to creep in. Several years into my marriage, I looked around and saw worldly passions eating away at my husband and me. I realized how difficult it had become to maintain my purity *within* my marriage. And I realized that my husband was struggling right along beside me, deeply affecting my own pursuit. Together we took a major "time-out" to just get before God and say, "OK, we see these worldly passions baring their razor-sharp teeth in our faces. We know they exist. Teach us to say no!"

Something happened. Slowly—painfully slowly—things began to change. My husband began to notice a difference in me, and I began to feel the difference. God began to work in me to teach me day by day the decisions and changes I needed to make to have a passionate marriage. The big difference was that now I had gotten real with God about how hopeless I was . . . library of marriage books and all . . . and I had begun to daily acknowledge that I still had a lot to learn.

When was the last time you simply uttered, "Lord, teach me"?
Won't you stop right now and ask Him to teach you as you read this book?

It's Your Turn

My story isn't unique. I'm just willing to tell it, dirty laundry and all. As I have been vulnerable, other women have become vulnerable with me, and I find that we all have quite a lot in common. You can read my story and listen to the stories of others I tell. I hope that gives you courage. But you must dig deeply into your own story for this book to be effective in your marriage.

Get a journal or notebook. You'll need it after you read each chapter in this book. Today, I want you to write a letter to God. Explain to Him where you are in your struggle to stand pure before Him. It could be any area of your life—language, anger, bitterness, depression, sexuality, romantic fantasizing, substance abuse—anything that is causing heartache in your life. Give each part of your history over to Him, no matter how old the pain or how new. Tell Him you are sorry if you have failed. Pray that He will keep you shielded from worldly passions. And specifically request Him to be your Teacher while you are reading this book.

Go ahead. Write!

OK, where we're headed next may seem a little basic, but sometimes you have to start at the beginning. So, before I get really transparent and let you see some of my own junk—and challenge you to see your own—we have to pinpoint the purpose of marriage. Join me for a basic, but mind-blowing, look at God's gift of physical intimacy. ■

"'For this reason a man will leave his father and

mother and be united to his wife, and the two will

become one flesh.' This is a profound mystery—

but I am talking about Christ and the church."

EPHESIANS 5:31–32

CHAPTER TWO

The Heavenly Purpose of Marriage

After just a few months of marriage, I still loved to mentally replay our first night together. I hoped in remembering it every day, I'd never be too far away from it to forget how special it was.

It had been amazing. It was tender and fulfilling, proof of our love. It was awkward and unperfected, proof of our innocence. Never, in all my life, had I felt so warm and comforted—as if the world had stopped around me simply so that I could really know and feel that moment.

Bob had moved away from me.

"No, don't go," I'd murmured, drawing him back to me.

He turned and kissed me tenderly on my nose, then proceeded to get out of bed. He tenderly and tightly wrapped me in the blankets and then knelt beside me. "Dannah, I want to pray," he said. "I want to thank God for this gift and beg His blessing upon our marriage bed that we might always protect it."

In just a few short months, I'd treasured that prayer as I'd already begun to see how much we were going to need it.

To understand marriage, you must understand the concept of covenant. Do you know what a covenant is? It's not a contract. It's not an agreement. A covenant is so much deeper and more honorable. Every time God does something significant in Scripture, He presents it as a covenant.

Let's dig a little deeper into this concept of covenant before we talk about what it has to do with your marriage. A covenant can be recognized by three specific characteristics.

1 A Covenant Is an *Unbreakable* Bond.

The Abrahamic covenant is a good example of a covenant that's unbreakable. God made a covenant with Abraham that would ensure Abraham's descendants would be as plentiful as the stars in the universe . . . an amazing promise for an old man who had no children. What did God do to Abraham's name after the covenant was made? He changed it from Abram to Abraham. Many Bible scholars believe that God was taking the H in His Hebrew name Yahweh and placing it within Abraham's name. Sarah's, too![1] It's also interesting that from that point on God refers to Himself, and others refer to Him, as the "God of Abraham." They were bonded to each other in a permanent sense, having been reidentified to acknowledge the unending relationship.

2 A Covenant Is Always Sealed in *Blood*.

Imagine being an old, wrinkled man who's very set in his ways when God shows up with the brilliant idea of . . . circumcision. Ouch! You have to wonder if Abraham didn't think more than twice about that. And yet, as much as we know about Abraham's doubting God and His promise several times (hiding Sarah's identity in Egypt and having sex with Hagar to "help God out"), we don't have any record of hesitation about the idea of circumcision. This is because Abraham knew the power of the presence of blood. Every covenant in Scripture is sealed in blood.

Noah's rainbow was sealed in blood at the base through an animal sacrifice.

Old Testament characters had to shed animal blood to receive forgiveness of sins. Christ shed His own blood to forgive us of our sins, wiping out Old Testament sacrifices. Blood is present in every biblical covenant. The blood is the "ink" of the covenant. It seals it.

3 A Covenant Is Followed by *Blessings* in the Form of an If/Then Agreement.

Covenants are made between a greater and a lesser party—in the Bible usually a monarch and his subjects or God and man. The greater party offers great gifts or blessings if the lesser party sticks to the agreement.

If Abraham would enter into the covenant of circumcision, *then* God would make his descendants like the stars of the universe. If Old Testament characters participated in animal sacrifice, *then* God would forgive their sins. If you and I embrace the blood of Jesus Christ as payment for our sins, *then* God forgives our sins and offers us eternal life.

Marriage Is a Blood Covenant

So, how does the marriage relationship line up with the requirements of a biblical blood covenant? Well, it has a lot to do with the beautiful gift of sexuality. In fact, without sex, I don't think you have the covenant of marriage. Let's look at it.

THE SECRET TRADITION OF COVENANT!

THE OLD TESTAMENT USES THE WORD *BERIYTH* FOR COVENANT. IT MEANT THAT A SOLEMN AGREEMENT HAD BEEN MADE BY PASSING THROUGH PIECES OF FLESH. THE TWO PARTIES ENTERING INTO THE COVENANT WOULD WALK BETWEEN THE PARTS OF A SACRIFICIAL ANIMAL, WHICH HAD BEEN TORN INTO TWO PIECES.

BEFORE I LOSE YOU WITH ALL THIS GORY, HISTORIC HEBREW STUFF, LET ME ASK YOU SOMETHING: DID YOU HAVE A TRADITIONAL WEDDING WHERE THE GROOM'S FAMILY SAT ON ONE SIDE OF THE CHURCH AND THE BRIDE'S ON THE OTHER? GUESS WHAT! THAT'S *BERIYTH* IN ACTION! THE JEWISH WEDDING CEREMONY STARTED THAT CUSTOM, AND MANY TRADITIONAL WEDDINGS STILL CONTAIN THAT BEAUTIFUL SPIRITUAL PORTRAIT FOR US. IT GOES OVER MOST OF OUR HEADS AS JUST SOME STUFFY TRADITION, BUT IT IS SO MUCH MORE MEANINGFUL. ■

1 Marriage Is a Covenant That Is an Unbreakable Bond.

God refers to the marriage relationship throughout Scripture as a covenant. In several places, He gives us His expectations that it should not be broken. For example, in Proverbs, He is grieved because a woman has "left the husband and ignored the covenant of her youth." God is grieved because He expected that marriage covenant, like every other covenant, to be honored as an unbreakable bond.

When I married Bob, I became Dannah Gresh. Just like Abraham was permanently identified with God by his name change, so am I . . . and proud of it! No matter where Bob goes geographically, spiritually, emotionally, or mentally, I am bonded to him. And he to me.

2 Marriage Is a Covenant That Is Sealed in Blood.

As you probably know, when a virgin bride has sexual intercourse for the very first time, there is usually a small issue of blood. This occurs when the hymen, a thin membrane inside her vagina, is stretched or torn. The hymen is one of a few tissues in the human body that medical science cannot quite figure out. They cannot identify any known purpose of the tissue. It's quite possible that God was checking off His list of requirements for covenants when He sealed the covenant of marriage with blood through the hymen.

In Bible times this was taken very seriously. The bride and groom were presented with white linens on their wedding night. They were expected to provide proof of the young woman's virginity on those linens. (Yikes! Thank You, Lord, for creating me to be a woman of the new millennium!)

Marriage is a covenant that is sealed in blood.

"CHRIST CLEARLY STATES IN MATTHEW 19:5 THAT 'THEY TWO SHALL BE ONE FLESH.' THE WEDDING CEREMONY IN ITSELF IS NOT THE ACT THAT REALLY UNITES A COUPLE IN HOLY MATRIMONY IN THE EYES OF GOD; IT MERELY GRANTS THEM THE PUBLIC LICENSE TO RETREAT PRIVATELY TO SOME ROMANTIC SPOT TO EXPERIENCE THE 'ONE FLESH' RELATIONSHIP THAT TRULY UNITES THEM AS HUSBAND AND WIFE."[2]

—TIM AND BEVERLY LAHAYE

---

3 Marriage Is a Covenant That Is Followed by Blessings in the Form of an If/Then Agreement.

Marriage is a covenant that is followed by three specific blessings of sexuality, which we'll look at in the next chapter. And remember, God's plan requires us to wait until we are married to indulge our sexual desires in any way whatsoever and then to jealously protect our marriage bed.

At the Last Supper Christ said, "If I go and prepare a place for you, I will come back and take you to be with me" That zooms right over our heads. It has no meaning to us, but to the disciples it was a clear and powerful picture.

You see, in those days when a young Jewish man wanted to marry a young Jewish woman, he had to go ask her dad for her hand in marriage. The groom-wannabe had to not only ask for his bride's hand, but also to prove he was worthy by providing some sort of payment. Sometimes it was a cow or two. If he had nothing of value, he would offer a few years of labor. After the payment was made, the groom had to go prepare a home. This could take months or years. He had to have the materials and time to build. He usually added a room onto his father's house. Sometimes he built his own house if he could afford it. As the construction was complete, the excitement grew because the *moment* it was finished the groom and his friends marched through the streets whooping and hollering as they moved toward the bride's home. No matter when it was . . . noon or three in the morning . . . he would return for his faithfully waiting bride the moment he'd completed his home. After all, he had "paid the price" and "prepared a place" for her.

See the picture? Do you see Christ paying for us just like the young man paid for the girl? Do you see Christ ascending into heaven to "prepare a place for us" just as the young man went to build a home for his bride? And one day our Savior will return again when we least expect it, just like the young man returned for his bride as soon as his home was ready for her.

Many times God gives us physical portraits so that we can understand great spiritual truths. The intimacy of pure sex is so intense that it is compared to the unfathomable love of Christ for His church. This is significant.

My friend, pure sex with your husband is the great physical example of Christ's intense love for you and me! Sex is separated and exalted as the portrait of the greatest spiritual truth that you and I know.

What motivation for Satan to distort this truth in your life! How he wants you to water down the intensity of sex so you cannot understand the passion Christ has for you! How he seeks to make your marriage a broken example of this powerful portrait! How he wants to ruin this gift for you.

Maybe he's had some success in the past. Maybe you are having a hard time understanding or believing this because you haven't experienced it in marriage. Hang in there, my friend. I think I have some hope for you, but first we need to finish our little sex talk.

All of this has been pretty heady, but we need to understand the heavenly purpose of sex. Sex really is out of this world! Now, let's get on with those three blessings as we bring sex down to earth.

"THE BIBLE'S REFERENCE TO THE CHURCH AS THE 'BRIDE OF CHRIST' IS A POWERFUL AND VIVID SYMBOLISM. SEXUAL ONENESS BETWEEN A HUSBAND AND A WIFE IS LIKE THE ONENESS BETWEEN GOD AND HIS PEOPLE."[3]

⌐ED YOUNG

It's Your Turn

Grab your journal and Bible. Turn to Ephesians 5:31–32. You're going to write a letter to God. In it I want you to reflect upon how you have seen the mystery in your marriage. Was there one time when you felt such unity in your marriage that it reflected the "mysterious" relationship of Christ and the church? Reflect on that time and ask the Lord to help you create more moments like that. ■

NOTES
1. Kay Arthur, *Our Covenant God* (Colorado Springs: Waterbrook, 1999), 171.
2. Tim and Beverly LaHaye, *The Act of Marriage* (Grand Rapids: Zondervan, 1976), 12.
3. Ed Young, *Pure Sex* (Sisters, Oreg.: Multnomah, 1997), 87.

"May your fountain be blessed, and may you rejoice

in the wife of your youth. A loving doe, a graceful deer—

may her breasts satisfy you always, may you ever

*be **intoxicated by her sex.**"*

PROVERBS 5:18–19

(The bold italics are my paraphrase based
*on the **actual Hebrew** language!)*

CHAPTER THREE

The Earthly Purpose of Marriage

I sat there trying to put my marriage into context. Exactly what did God want me to do with this relationship? I sat back against the soft pillows in my bed and imagined the first man sitting in the beauty of Eden.

"Let's see . . ." sighed Adam, leaning back in the grass to admire the animal's sleek black-and-white stripes.

"You will be called . . ." he began for what seemed like the zillionth time. "Let's see . . . I've only got one letter left. Zzzzz . . ."

"Zebra," boomed a Great Voice from behind him. "It will be called Zebra."

"Oh, God! That's funny. I was just about to say the same thing," exclaimed Adam as he breathed a sigh of relief. "Well, that about does it."

"Adam?" questioned the thunderous voice. "Do you know why I asked you to name the animals?"

"Well, they needed names, I guess," answered the man matter-of-factly.

"Adam!" challenged the Great Voice. *"Do you not know that I perceived your idea for each animal before you even discovered its existence? Could I not have placed their names into you in a moment just as I did the other knowledge that you have?"*

Adam sat up with a dumbfounded look of surprise. He hadn't considered that during the long process of studying, analyzing, and naming. He felt a little foolish. He ran a hand through his already mussed hair and turned with a puzzled look in the direction of the Great Voice.

"Adam, what did you feel?" asked the Voice.

"Well . . . uh . . . feel? . . ." he stuttered, searching for an answer.

"Close your eyes, Man," encouraged the Voice. "Tell me what you felt when you named the animals."

He lay back into the grass and closed his eyes.

The ache returned.

It was the same ache he'd felt when he'd seen the playful lioness prancing around the lion. It was the same ache he'd felt when he watched the ducks waddling together, beak-to-tail, everywhere they went. It was the same ache he'd felt when he'd heard the giant tortoises roaring for each other.

"It hurts," admitted Adam.

"Where?" questioned the Great Voice.

"Here," sighed Adam as he grasped his flesh-covered rib cage.

There was a silent pause.

The ache suddenly throbbed more deeply as an invisible hand reached into the man's body.

Adam slipped out of consciousness.

Flesh ripped.

Bone cracked.

When he awakened, his vision was blurred. The sun's rays danced through his lashes. He lay there unable to imagine ever getting up.

And then, he heard it.

It was a voice. A voice as welcoming and as warm as the Great Voice but higher, sweeter. It was singing like the birds. He willed himself to rise. He contracted his stomach muscles to sit up, grimacing at a tenderness where the ache had once been.

He held his side tenderly as he panned the landscape, searching for the source of this sweet sound. He pushed himself up and stood looking toward the sound. His eyes stopped at the movement under the waterfall.

"Ohhhh!" he barely breathed as his eyes received the first glimpse of . . . what

was this? He looked upon the curves of a creature so elegant and so beautiful. . . . Had he missed one?

Forgetting his discomfort, he stumbled into the water to get closer, clumsily splashing through the ripples of wetness.

The creature turned at the noise.

"Ohhhhhh, great beauty!" bellowed the man, skidding to a stop. His eyes gazed fully upon the unique, sculptured beauty of the creature before him. His mind raced. His pulse quickened. His skin released cold liquid.

The ache.

Oh, the ache!

The sweet, sweet ache!

It was deeper, lower . . . different. It was no longer hurting, but hopeful. It was no longer dull with deadness but alive with longing. It wasn't pulling him within but pushing him to reach out.

He stumbled forward to touch the beauty . . . to absorb the smell . . . to consume the sweet presence.

"You shall be called Woman," he whispered as he reached her.

From the edge of the water, the Great Voice whispered, "You are no longer alone, my Man friend."

We just learned that marriage is a covenant, and a big part of the covenant is the sexual blessings or benefits that follow if that covenant is enjoyed according to God's plan. The covenant of sexuality has three great benefits.

Benefit Number One: Sex Is a Spiritual Portrait That Enhances Intimacy

Dr. John Gottman, best-selling author of *The Seven Principles for Making Marriage Work*, reports, "The determining factor in whether wives feel satisfied with sex is, by 70 percent, the quality of the couple's friendship. For men, the determining factor is, by 70 percent, the quality of friendship." [1] He points to the emotional bond that must exist for sex to be truly fulfilling. Satisfying sex is not the result of buff bodies and powerful sex drives. It is the result of an emotional bond . . . a deep friendship.

Something that helps me get this into my head is the idea that Adam was alone before Eve was created. Here's Adam hangin' in the garden. He was sinless. He had no guilt or shame or fear to deal with. And yet, God looked at him and realized that it wasn't good for him to be alone. Everything else in the garden was good . . . everything. But it was *not* good that Adam was alone. *Alone?* God Himself was walking and talking with Adam. Alone? How could he be alone?

God could have filled that loneliness Himself. He didn't. Adam would not be complete until God created Eve. His loneliness would not be voided until Eve was present. Imagine that!

Now don't get the wrong idea here. Sex *alone* doesn't create intimacy. Sex outside of commitment can actually ruin a relationship . . . and potentially relationships to come, including the one with your husband. Sexual sin gets in the way of the emotional and spiritual parts of the marriage relationship and creates discomfort, shame, and a lack of intimacy.

Author Heather Jamison gives these letters from women who'd had premarital sex.

"It took us nearly ten years to rework how we thought about sex so that we could enjoy it."

"Nathan and I have been married for almost ten years and it was only last summer that I finally realized that making love to my husband was something that actually brought God joy. Talk about a revelation. . . . My whole idea of sex, the way God really designed it, had been altered because of what was done prior to this union."[2]

Even if the man you are married to was the one you had sex with prior to your wedding night, you might be running into similar frustration. At a retreat for college-age women that I spoke at a few years ago, a married mentor stood up to say through tears: "Girls, please wait. My husband and I love each other very much, and we are committed to each other, but our sex life is terrible because I can't get over the shame of having sex with him before we were married."

Maybe you know what I'm talking about. Oh, I hope not, but if you do there is healing and hope to know that intimacy. Keep reading. We're building upon God's Word truth by truth.

The truth I want you to see right now is that protected purity enhances intimacy through a holy sexual experience. *Pure sex enhances intimacy.*

Benefit Number Two:
Sex Creates Life

Genesis 1:28 issues an early command for us to populate the earth . . . to make babies! Robby came into this world exactly fifteen months after our wedding. Lexi joined our little family three and a half years later. And every single day of both of those pregnancies was a celebration. I remember (with a bit of a blush now) a particularly odd moment of celebration when I had Lexi. I had the privilege of delivering her naturally even though Robby had been a C-section. I went to the doctors for a cold, and four hours later she'd pretty much just popped out . . . not much pain and no painkillers. Ha! What a way to have a baby! An hour after her birth, they took her away and took me to the shower room to be sponged down by a loving nurse. Under normal circumstances I'd have been a bit embarrassed, but not on this day. I remember standing there thinking, *Wow! Hey, open the doors to this bathroom and invite everyone in. They've got to see this body of mine. It's just done the most amazing thing!* I didn't do it, though. My senses took hold of me, and I just smiled as the nurse scrubbed away!

The incredible gift of creating life is the most God-like thing you or I can do. When experienced within the marriage union, it provides unparalleled moments of celebration. Certainly, babies have been conceived outside of marriage time and time again. But the gift is so amazing; it deserves to be unmarred and undistracted by bad timing.

Pure sex creates babies with great celebration.

DOES THIS HURT YOU?

MAYBE YOU ARE FEELING HURT AND FRUSTRATED READING THIS BECAUSE YOU HAVEN'T EXPERIENCED THE BLESSINGS. WORSE YET, MAYBE YOU'VE EXPERIENCED JUST THE OPPOSITE. MAYBE SEXUAL INTIMACY HAS BEEN REPLACED WITH AWKWARDNESS AND SHAME. MAYBE THE JOY OF HAVING BABIES WAS REPLACED WITH STRUGGLING TO CELEBRATE THE BEAUTIFUL LIFE OF YOUR CHILD DESPITE BAD TIMING. MAYBE SEX IS NO FUN AT ALL FOR YOU.

GOD WANTS YOU TO HAVE A FANTASTIC, FUN SEXUAL RELATIONSHIP THAT'S MORE THAN YOU CAN EVEN IMAGINE. EVEN IF THERE HAS BEEN SEXUAL MISUSE IN YOUR OR YOUR HUSBAND'S PAST, YOU CAN KNOW THE FULL FORGIVENESS AND RESTORATION OF THIS GIFT, THOUGH IT MAY TAKE A LITTLE EXTRA WORK. STICK WITH ME ON THIS! BY THE END OF THE BOOK, I HOPE TO GIVE YOU SPECIFIC STEPS TO TAKE TO FOLLOW HEALING AND OPEN UP THE DOORS TO FABULOUS INTIMACY WITH YOUR HUSBAND. ■

Benefit Number Three:
Sex Is Sheer Pleasure

Proverbs 5:18–19 says, "May your fountain be blessed, and may you rejoice in the wife of your youth. A loving doe, a graceful deer—may her breasts satisfy you always, may you ever be captivated by her love."

I was sitting in a Burger King interviewing Josh McDowell for my first book, *And the Bride Wore White,* when he quoted that verse to me and then asked, "Dannah, do you take the Bible literally?" I didn't have a clue what to say to this man who knows the Word of God inside and out. I sat in stunned silence. Then, a big grin played across his face and he said, "When I read this verse, I sure like to take the Bible literally!" We enjoyed a good laugh, and then he really challenged me on this issue of celebrating God's gift of sexual pleasure.

In the book of Deuteronomy, God says basically that He knows we are going to wonder why He has placed guidelines for living upon us. He doesn't want us to wonder what they are all about, so He says right out several times that the purpose of them is to make us "prosper." He wants us to prosper . . . that includes sexually. He doesn't ask us to wait to have sex to torture us. He knows that if we wait, it will be far more fantastic.

Social science proves this today. A recent sex study entitled "Sex in America" was conducted with a relatively liberal agenda, but page 124 of the layman's version of that study says, "People who reported being the most physically pleased and emotionally satisfied [with sex] were the married couples." It went on to say that "the lowest rates of satisfaction were among men and women who were neither married nor living with someone—the very group thought to be having the hottest sex." Furthermore, "physical and emotional satisfaction started to decline when people had more than one

TAKE IT A STEP FURTHER

TIM AND BEVERLY LaHAYE SURVEYED 3,377 CHRISTIAN COUPLES TO LEARN ABOUT THEIR SEX LIVES. ACCORDING TO THEM, THE COUPLES WHO PRAYED TOGETHER REGULARLY WERE MORE THAN 10 PERCENT MORE LIKELY TO HAVE A "VERY HAPPY/ABOVE AVERAGE" SEX LIFE THAN THOSE WHO DID NOT PRAY TOGETHER.[3] WHY? BECAUSE GOD LOVES TO BE IN THE VERY CENTER OF A VIBRANT MARRIAGE RELATIONSHIP, AND HE OFTEN BLESSES THAT WITH THE GREAT PHYSICAL GIFT OF SEXUAL SATISFACTION. I BET YOU'RE OFF TO PRAY WITH YOUR HUSBAND RIGHT NOW, AREN'T YOU! ∎

sexual partner."[4] Science today proves what God said hundreds of years ago. When we wait to have sex with one man, it can be fantastic!

Pure sex is a blast!

I think the whole story of sexuality is so romantic, but before this story starts sounding like a happily-ever-after fairy tale, I'd like to introduce you to the villain. I've faced him. He's played a big role in my story. He's probably been in yours somewhere even if you don't realize it. Introducing . . . the Adversary.

It's Your Turn

Write a love note to your husband . . . a risqué, fun note! Include Proverbs 5:18–19 and tell him that you are truly excited about the fact that God wants you to enjoy each other like this. (Make sure you have time to enjoy the response when you give it to him.)

NOTES

1. John M. Gottman and Nan Silver, *The Seven Principles for Making Marriage Work* (New York: Three Rivers Press, 1999), 17.
2. Heather Jamison, *Reclaiming Intimacy* (Grand Rapids: Kregel, 2001), 79.
3. Tim and Beverly LaHaye, *The Act of Marriage* (Grand Rapids: Zondervan, 1976), 209.
4. Robert T. Michael, John H. Gagnon, Edward O. Laumann, and Gina Kolata, *Sex in America* (New York: Warner, 1994), 124.

"The devil . . . was a murderer from the beginning,

not holding to the truth, for there is no truth in

him. When he lies, he speaks his native language,

for he is a liar and the father of lies."

CHAPTER FOUR

The Enemy of Marriage

Why hadn't he come? *He should be here by now. I'd left our bed hysterical. I fully expected him to follow me. Why hadn't he? I'd waited and waited for him to come.*

Maybe he was hurting too. Maybe he just didn't know what to say. Maybe if I just showed myself, we'd fall into each other's arms and everything would be OK.

The clock ticked slowly. I waited a half hour, then I walked into our bedroom to see if maybe he was hurt too.

My jaw dropped. There he was doing the unthinkable. I couldn't imagine him doing anything more thoughtless. But there he lay . . .

. . . sleeping.

How could he?

Where was the joy in this marriage?

Wasn't marriage supposed to make me happy?

or just a moment, place yourself in the great play of humanity. The playbill credits you as The Adversary. Your character's goal is to destroy the universe, which can be accomplished only by cutting off all contact between The Savior, Christ, and Humanity, played by households and households of humans.

You need to get into your role here, horrible as it is. (Are you uncomfortable with this? You should be. But stick with me for a minute. I really want you to see something from a new point of view. I think it'll be worth our shared discomfort for a few brief moments.)

As your acting coach, I challenge you to think like the Adversary. How will you do it—corrupt the universe? Do you lock 'em up and throw away the key? No, the Savior would come running to the rescue of Humanity. Do you show up looking demonic and frightening? No, Humanity would run to the Savior.

Think harder.

Ahhhh, yes! That's it. You'll make Humanity completely unable to understand this Savior's very character. They won't miss what they can't comprehend. Now, how exactly does the Savior actively show Himself to Humanity today? What's one of the most powerful portraits of His love? Ah, yes. Of course. *That's* the target. If they can't understand *marriage*, they'll struggle to understand the Savior's passion for them.

You dress in your camouflage and you gather your first microscopic bomb.

It's so small, it's imperceptible. They won't even notice when it's there, you think to yourself with a nasty little grin.

You point to the world and slowly close in on the target.

Yes, this home will do.

You'll start with this house . . . but wait!

Oh, no!

Do you recognize that wedding portrait in the window?

Hold it!

Abort this fictional mission . . . that's your home!

. . . your marriage is the target!

Know this, my friend. Satan knows all too well that the most powerful portrait of Christ's passion is a pure and holy marriage. As Christians continue to misuse sex and succumb to divorce, the whole world comes to understand less of who God is because we understand less of His love as it was meant for us to know it within a faithful, loving, passionate marriage.

Understanding this has brought a whole new expectation to my marriage. I used to think that my marriage was supposed to make me *happy*. But I've learned that the purpose of marriage is *not* to make me happy.

It's to make me *holy*.

Let's look at what it portrays a little more closely. Is the purpose of your relationship with Christ to make you happy? No. The ultimate purpose of your relationship with Christ is to make you holy . . . to prepare you to live in constant, eternal communion with a holy God.

In fact, Christ's gift to us is the Holy Spirit. His job? Not to make you comfortable, though he is the Comforter. Funny thing, that role as Comforter is a necessity since most of the time He is making us very uncomfortable.

Think I'm off base here? Just look at Matthew 4. We've just witnessed the baptism of Christ and the beautiful descending of God's Holy Spirit onto Christ in the form of a dove. In Matthew 4:1, we see the Holy Spirit starting His job when the Word says, "Then Jesus was led by the Spirit into the desert to be tempted by the devil."

Yikes! The first job of the Holy Spirit was to make Christ very uncomfortable so that He could *display* the holiness of God. Holiness comes through the cleansing blood of Christ and the thorough work of the Holy Spirit. That often includes exposing us to discomfort so we can *develop* the Christlike character traits such as patience, love, goodness, kindness, faithfulness, and peace. The purpose of the work of Christ and the Holy Spirit is to make you and me holy.

If your marriage is a portrait of that relationship, it certainly makes sense that the purpose of it is not to make you happy but to aid the Spirit in developing holiness in you.

Ever feel like your marriage is driving you into the desert of temptation?

Temptation to speak harshly and unkindly?

Temptation to manipulate your own way?

Temptation to look for affection outside of your marriage?

Temptation to make fun of your husband in front of your friends?

Temptation to look back at the past and bring it up as a weapon?

I could go on.

I don't know about you, but when it comes to this part of the portrait of marriage . . . I qualify! Do you? Then, be glad that the Savior stands ready to play His role . . . to rescue you.

But first you have to see exactly what it is you need to be rescued from so you can call out to Him. I wish it were easy to see strongholds in our lives. It's

> "THERE IS NO NEUTRAL GROUND IN THE UNIVERSE. EVERY SQUARE INCH, EVERY SPLIT SECOND IS CLAIMED BY GOD AND COUNTERCLAIMED BY SATAN."
> ⸻C. S. LEWIS, *The Weight of Glory*

not. The Adversary is so clever and deceptive. He places truly microscopic impurities in our lives. We don't face snarling demons or hateful acts of physical persecution on a daily basis. Instead, the Adversary crafts alluring and seemingly innocent counterfeit valuables for us to "buy." Subtly and passively, we find ourselves investing in these "fake pearls" rather than in the precious relationship Jesus Christ offers us. Quite often we don't even see the danger.

It happens to the best of us. It happened to King David, someone the Bible says was "a man after God's own heart." In 1 Chronicles 21:1 we read that "Satan rose up against Israel and incited David to take a census of Israel."

Clever little scheme the Adversary had here! The act of counting the armies of God was *so close* to stewardship. But God did not want the armies counted. He did not want a growing army to take credit for the victories when the credit for them belonged to God.

David counted away, thinking himself a good steward of God's armies. And Satan stood at the door of stewardship, laughing away with his little side-kick Pride at his side. Chalk one up for the Adversary.

Sadly, God punished Israel by destroying many of those men the king counted. If David can fall so passively, can't you? Can't I? How can we break Satan's bondage in our marriage if we can't even see it?

Neil Anderson, author of *The Bondage Breaker*, writes,

You wonder, "Am I doomed in my dilemma? I have left the door open for Satan, and he has taken advantage of my spiritual passivity. Can I get him out of the places he has wormed into?" The answer is a resounding yes! Jesus Christ is the Bondage Breaker. But in order to experience His freedom, we must find the doors we left open through which Satan gained entrance.[1]

My friend, let's inspect a few doors together! I want you to be able to identify those fake pearls I've been talking about.

It's Your Turn

At a point when my marriage was more miserable than marvelous, a Christian counselor asked me to do something that was *very* uncomfortable for me. He asked me to write a letter to the devil. That's right! You read correctly. Let me explain.

This wonderful counselor pointed out that I'd been blaming everything and everyone . . . mostly my husband . . . for the hurt in my marriage, all the while denying that Satan was the ultimate cause of my hurt. (Remember Ephesians 6:12 tells us that our struggle is not against flesh and blood—and that *includes* your husband—but against "the rulers, against the authorities, against the powers of this dark world and against the spiritual forces of evil in the heavenly realms.")

In following through with my writing assignment, I was abandoning the bad habit of selfishly blaming my husband and I was rightfully identifying Satan as the cause of pain in my marriage.

I was both nervous and strangely empowered at the idea of writing this letter. I wrote it in the *name of Jesus* to tell Satan that the battle he'd waged against my marriage would not be won. I was pointing to him as my true Adversary and the source of my hurt. I was also calling upon the name of Jesus to be rescued. What a powerful exercise that was for me and a pivotal point of maturity in how I dealt with hurt in my marriage.

Although we must never become overly focused upon Satan nor look for opportunities to face him, it is not only biblical but wise to take a stand in the name of Jesus when we do face him. First Peter 5:8 says, "Be sober, be vigilant [in other words "wake up and stay awake"]; because your adversary the devil walks about like a roaring lion, seeking whom he may devour" (NKJV). James 4:7 and 1 Peter 5:9 both use the word *resist,* which means "to take a stand against." There's nothing passive about that. It's a position of power . . . *in the name of Jesus.*

I'd like to invite you to write a similar letter. In it you will (a) rightfully place the blame for hurt in your marriage on Satan and (b) clearly point to the power of God to rescue you. Don't even think of doing it unless you take on the task in the name of Jesus. Only in His name can we even face such evil. If you are a follower of Christ, don't be afraid to identify your true adversary and claim the blood of Jesus Christ against him. ■

NOTE
1. Neil T. Anderson, *The Bondage Breaker* (Eugene, Ore: Harvest House, 1993), 182.

CHAPTER FIVE

THE ENEMY'S FAKE PEARLS
Status & Stuff

He was here!

From inside our tiny little town house, I could see my husband reading the sign leading to the trail of pink Easter eggs. I watched as he followed the trail, opening the eggs one by one. Each one contained a written clue about the news I had to tell him.

Soon he burst through the back door with an inquisitive look on his face.

"Is it . . . ?" Bob stammered.

I plopped our two-and-a-half-year-old Robby up onto the kitchen table next to a pink cake I'd covered with pink marshmallow bunnies. Robby extended his chubby little fingers to give his daddy a bouquet of pink balloons.

"Are we . . . ?" he asked again.

"Yes!" I exclaimed. "You're going to be a daddy again!"

We laughed and cried and kissed Robby. We ate the pink cake and dreamed hopefully of a little girl.

That night we cuddled in bed and contemplated how we'd ever fit another baby into our 500-square-foot town house.

"You'll have a home by the time this baby is born," Bob said. "And you'll have a minivan too."

I hugged him. I didn't know how he'd ever pull that off with our business still in its infancy, but I believed he could do it.

Four months later we were in our first home.

One week before the baby was born, he handed me the keys to a brand-new white Dodge Caravan.

(And the pink cake worked!)

The Adversary stood outside my heart at the door of contentment. His little slave driver, Greed, gloated at their little victory.

his world offers us a lot of "good" things into which we can invest our time and energy. Oh, be careful. Investing in even the tiniest or perhaps most common of this world's fake treasures can mean giving up God's chosen treasure for you.

I'm reminded of my wedding day when I was faced with the choice of wearing the ornate costume pearl-drop earrings I'd searched for and treasured for so many weeks or wearing the simple but real, round pearl studs that my groom had chosen and presented to me on that day. To be truthful, I did pause to struggle with the choice. I'd envisioned that day with my hair up and my pearls dangling from my ears. But, oh, my groom had chosen these subtle treasures of greater value. Which would *I* choose? I chose the gift my groom offered on that day.

"DO ONLY UNBELIEVERS HAVE STRONGHOLDS?" ABSOLUTELY NOT! THE BOOK OF GALATIANS, THE NEW TESTAMENT'S PRIMARY TREATISE FOR FREEDOM, WAS ADDRESSED TO BELIEVERS IN GALATIA. GALATIANS 5:1 SAYS, "IT IS FOR FREEDOM THAT CHRIST HAS SET US FREE. STAND FIRM, THEN, AND DO NOT LET YOURSELVES BE BURDENED AGAIN BY A YOKE OF SLAVERY." LIKEWISE, 2 CORINTHIANS 10:3–5, WHICH ADDRESSES THE DEMOLITION OF STRONGHOLDS, WAS WRITTEN TO BELIEVERS. THE WORD IS VERY PRACTICAL. GOD NEVER ADDRESSES "NON-ISSUES." IF A BELIEVER COULD NOT RETURN TO A YOKE OF SLAVERY, HE WOULD NEVER HAVE WARNED US OF THE POTENTIALITY OF IT.[1] ■ ────►BETH MOORE

I wish I could say that the rest of my life exemplified such discernment for value, but I realize now that I so often surpass greater gifts—treasures that God has chosen for my life—to grasp onto this world's imposters. Investing in this world's fake pearls can result in a yoke of slavery so powerful that your life is drastically (yet often imperceptibly) controlled. The cost can be great. We never set out to be enslaved by strongholds, but they slowly creep in through innocent passivity.

Let's look at two fake pearls that we ladies love to wear together: status and stuff! The natural desire to have a home to call our own, a faithful car that gets us where we need to go, and even clothes that make us look presentable can ever-so-subtly become fake pearls in our lives. How?

Are You Exhausted from Working Too Much?

Overwork is the honored addiction. Instead of checking workaholics into a rehab center, we place them at the head tables of awards banquets. I'm not talking about honorable hard work. I'm talking about overworking.

For many years, my schedule usually included rising to get the kids off to school and day care, working through lunch, leaving at 3:00 so that I could be home with my kids until bedtime, cleaning the house and cooking while I was home, and then returning to the office as soon as the kids got to sleep so I could work until between midnight and two in the morning. I didn't set out to be a workaholic; I wanted to provide a home for my children. I was determined to be a Christian testimony in community clubs and organizations I attended. I desired to build a credible voice for Christian issues in my city through the monthly magazine and radio stations that we owned. I had all good intentions . . . or so it seemed. Yet all the while I'd been investing in this fake pearl of status. I was building up an expense account with Greed.

You don't have to work outside the home to overwork. You'll find a home-making workaholic right in the Bible. Her name is Martha. She focused so much on the cooking and cleaning that she forgot to sit at the feet of Jesus and was outright nasty to her sister for "not doing her share." Ever find yourself snapping at your husband for "not doing his share"?

Even something as commonplace as our kids' schedules can drive us into overworking. The expectation today is for our children to be in every sport and every special after-school or church activity from the moment they hit first grade. By the time they are teenagers, they have to be at school at

THE *700 CLUB'S* LISA RYAN ON WOMEN AND CAREERS

DANNAH: THE POSITION YOU ARE IN INFLUENCES SO MANY. DID YOU HAVE TO MAKE CHOICES . . . TOUGH CHOICES . . . TO BUILD CHARACTER BEFORE YOU WERE CALLED TO THAT POSITION?

LISA: AFTER HAVING BEEN MISS CALIFORNIA AND AS A YOUNG MARRIED WOMAN WITH NO CHILDREN—I WAS REALLY PURSUING A TV CAREER IN CALIFORNIA AND WAS JUST BEGINNING TO GET SOME SIGNIFICANT ROLES AND OPPORTUNITIES. DURING THAT TIME, I GOT PREGNANT WITH OUR FIRST CHILD, BUT CONTINUED PURSUING THAT WHOLE CAREER THING. A YEAR INTO DRAGGING OUR DAUGHTER OFF TO AUDITIONS WITH ME, I REALIZED, "I'M A MOTHER NOW. THAT HAS TO BE MY PRIORITY NOW. I CAN'T HAVE IT ALL NOW."

DANNAH: WHAT DID YOU DO AS A RESULT OF REALIZING THAT?

LISA: I WALKED AWAY FROM THE CAREER COMPLETELY, BUT THAT DREAM DIED A SLOW, PAINFUL DEATH.

DANNAH: DID THAT HURT?

LISA: IT DID HURT. IN MY IGNORANCE AND IMMATURITY, I THOUGHT, *THAT'S IT! MY LIFE'S OVER. GOD'S NEVER GONNA USE*

(continued on page 49 . . .)

6:45 A.M. because all of the "after-school" activities no longer fit after school. Often after they're done with that after-school stuff, they head off to an evening job before coming home late to cram some studying into the day. It's too much.

Let me speak my heart and say just two words: That's unholy!

Again, I'm not talking about teaching our kids a healthy level of responsibility and involvement. I'm talking about over-committing them . . . and you, since you usually pay in the form of gasoline bills and exhaustion.

Step back with me to the book of Exodus where God established the Ten Commandments of our lives. Peek at the verse right there in the middle of "Don't worship another God" and "Don't commit adultery" and "Don't kill." See that lo-o-o-o-o-ng one. (God must have wanted to really get the point across on this one.) It says,

"Remember the Sabbath day by keeping it holy. Six days you shall labor and do all your work, but the seventh day is a Sabbath to the LORD your God. On it you shall not do any work, neither you, nor your son or daughter, nor your manservant or maidservant, nor your animals, nor the alien within your gates. For in six days the LORD made the heavens and the earth, the sea, and all that is in them, but he rested on the seventh day. Therefore the LORD blessed the Sabbath day and made it holy."

(EXODUS 20:8–11)

We sure like to throw that one out with the "law." But we don't throw out the other stuff. The ones about adultery, thievery, murder. We'll keep those!

"NO ONE WHO IS IN FINANCIAL BONDAGE CAN BE SPIRITUALLY FREE."
⟶ LARRY BURKETT

Come on! God must have thought that your rest was important. Very important. He put it right there on His list of the top ten when He said, "Do rest!" Maybe it won't be on the "Sabbath," but you must have rest in your life.

You might be saying, "Dannah, I have a really good reason for working so hard."

Yeah, and I bet I know what it is.

Do You *Have* to Work Because of the Payments You Must Make Each Month?

A fellow preschool mom and I were picking up our daughters one day. This lady was supermom if I ever saw it. She sold real estate; her husband was a well-paid and locally well-known politician. They lived in a neighborhood with doctors and lawyers. They had a beautiful, big home. But as our girls played that day, I asked her how she was doing and saw the other side of the story.

"I'm so tired," she said. "I'm working most evenings and weekends, so I don't get much time at home with my family, and when I am there I have so much to do."

"Do you like your job?" I asked.

(continued from page 48 . . .)

ME AGAIN. I'M EMBARRASSED TO ADMIT THAT AS A DAUGHTER OF THE FEMINIST MOVEMENT, I DIDN'T VALUE MOTHERHOOD. I WAS DISAPPOINTED FEELING LIKE MAYBE I HADN'T DONE ALL THAT I SHOULD HAVE DONE CAREER-WISE BEFORE I ENTERED THIS SEASON OF MY LIFE. I FELT LIKE A TV CAREER WASN'T MEANT TO BE ANYMORE.

DANNAH: YOU LET GO OF THE DREAM?

LISA: YEAH, I PUT IT ON THE SHELF LIKE AN UNFINISHED BOOK AND TOLD GOD IF IT EVER CAME DOWN HE WOULD HAVE TO DO THAT. I THREW MYSELF INTO MOTHERHOOD AND MY MARRIAGE.

DANNAH: WHAT DIFFERENCES DID YOU SEE IN YOUR MARRIAGE/FAMILY?

LISA: I USED TO THINK I WOULD FIND CONTENTMENT "DOING IT ALL" AND "BEING IT ALL." I THOUGHT IT WOULD COME IN ALL OF THE PROFESSIONAL ACCOMPLISHMENTS THAT WOULD BRING RECOGNITION . . . THE TROPHY THINGS. TO MY SURPRISE, I WAS MOST CONTENT WHEN I LET GO OF THOSE THINGS. I EMBRACED WHERE I WAS AT THE MOMENT . . . I DIDN'T KNOW THE FUTURE AND I STOPPED STRIVING. I WAS MUCH MORE AT PEACE AS A PERSON, AS A WOMAN WHEN I FINALLY RESTED IN IT. I FINALLY FOUND THE CONTENTEDNESS THAT I WAS ALWAYS LOOKING FOR. ■

"No, not really," she answered.

"What's keeping you from quitting to slow down and enjoy your family?" I asked her.

"A huge mortgage payment," she told me honestly.

Her debt was shackling her to workaholism.

Debt does that. It shackles us to a lifestyle that's not healthy. But debt is "normal" in our society. We're expected to have and use credit cards. We thoughtlessly sign loans for cars that are loaded with all the options. We consider it the "all-American dream" to have a mortgage payment. We've been reprogrammed to live by a code that normalizes debt. And slowly we become slaves to our finances.

Look what the Bible says about living according to the normalized debt structure of today's society and striving for wealth.

"Do not be a man who strikes hands in pledge or puts up security for debts; if you lack the mans to pay, your very bed will be snatched from under you."
(PROVERBS 22:26–27)

"Do not wear yourself out to get rich; have the wisdom to show restraint."
(PROVERBS 23:4)

Don't fall for this world's lie that debt is OK. It's not. It's just a way to get things that won't ever really satisfy you. Oh, how I wish I'd had that wisdom ten years ago. It would have saved me a lot of days of painfully paying for our debt . . . both financially and emotionally. I'll let you have a peek into my heart on that later on, but for now let's get back to the way our culture normalizes things. There are a couple of other things this culture offers us that are quite costly fake pearls, but they are camouflaged as innocent pastimes. Let's take a peek at our world of entertainment.

It's Your Turn

Two powerful tools will reveal Satan's slimy schemes to you . . . prayer and the Bible. We'll talk more about them later on. For right now, let's get them out and use them a little at the end of a few of these chapters. Won't you pray right now to ask God to reveal to you if workaholism or debt is knocking at the door of contentment?

Here's a Scripture prayer I wrote for you. Take a moment and pray it, or, better yet, write it into your journal. Add to it as the Spirit leads you.

Lord, show me if I am overworking to become rich. Give me understanding to slow down if I need to. Help me not to set my eyes on the deceptive things of this world like homes and cars and clothes and vacations. Your Word says that riches will make wings for themselves and fly away. (BASED ON PROVERBS 23:4–5)

Lord, I know that because of laziness, a home will decay, and through idleness of hands the house will fall apart. Show me if I am struggling with slothfulness. Make me a good steward of what You have given to me. (BASED ON ECCLESIASTES 10:18)

Your Word says that the blessings of the Lord make one rich and that You'll add no sorrow with it. When You provide for me financially, it leads to contentment. Reveal to me where there might be sorrow because of the way I chase after things on my own power. Give me a balanced perspective on work, for I know that for every person to whom God has given riches and wealth, You've also given us the power to eat of it and to receive it as a heritage. (BASED ON PROVERBS 10:22; ECCLESIASTES 5:19)

Whoa! Did you pray those verses or just skip over them? I'll warn you now that if you skip the Bible verse prayers, you'll be missing the most powerful part of this book.

NOTE
1. Beth Moore, *Praying God's Word* (Nashville: Broadman & Holman, 2000), 11.

CHAPTER SIX

THE ENEMY'S FAKE PEARLS:
Social Acceptance

I sat watching Good Will Hunting *with my husband next to me devouring a bag of butter-soaked popcorn. We rarely missed a good movie, but not many were this absorbing. Every line was perfectly written. I didn't want it to end. But it did.*

I stood and turned to leave. There behind me were three girls from our youth group, and my husband and I were youth leaders.

Suddenly the vivid joke about oral sex and the number of times the "f-word" was spoken ran through my mind. I saw the casual sex scenes in mental replay.

I thought it was terrible that these kids were allowed to see this movie. But then, I was there with them, wasn't I?

"Hey, guys," I said after a few moments of small talk. "I just have to apologize for watching this movie in front of you. It was really rough and I'm sorry."

"What was bad about it?" one of the girls asked.

"Yeah, we didn't think it was so bad," said another.

"We've seen much, much worse," the third chimed in.

I drove home that night dumbfounded. I wasn't just

upset about what I'd exposed myself to. I was upset that those girls had seen me exposing myself to it. How did I get this far? I wondered.

There he was again, though I couldn't see him through the clutter. The Adversary stood analyzing me with his longtime gangster, Oppression.

*O*ppression. It means to dominate. It's the goal of persecution. We expect persecution to involve verbal ridicule, extreme embarrassment, and great physical harm. To this day, Christians in other countries risk their lives for Christ. The intention of that kind of persecution is to so dominate us physically that it snuffs out our faith. Ironically, that kind of open persecution often creates empathy, camaraderie, and resistance.

You and I face an entirely different kind of oppression in our modern world. I believe it is far more deadly because it so effectively snuffs out the burning passion of our faith. Author Kenneth A. Myers says that "every generation of Christians faces unique challenges. . . . The challenges of living with popular culture may well be as serious for modern Christians as persecution and plagues were for the saints of earlier centuries."[1]

Why should Satan beat devotion to Christ out of us, when we take ourselves out with our own eyes? We do it every day when we become absorbed into the norm of our culture. Oppression is no longer some nasty, frightening beast but a popular pastime as our minds are dominated subtly and often with humor. (Stick with me here. If you're feeling uncomfortable with where I am headed, let me say that I've been there too! But let's stretch together!)

Are You Going Along with the Crowd's Popular Choices for Entertainment?

We think we are above it all. We think that we can take it in but not be altered or affected by it. After all, "the sex scene was short" and "I don't use that language" and "it's just humor." Are you above it all? Are you truly not affected by it?

Television executive Ted Turner says you are very much affected by what you see on TV. He says "everything we're exposed to influences us. . . . Films influence us, and the TV programs we see influence us. The weaker your family is, the more they influence you."[2]

We live in a new age of TV. Voyeurism is the rage. Recently in my

Sunday school class we discussed the show *Temptation Island,* which featured four "committed" but unmarried couples who went to an island together to test their faithfulness. Once they arrived, they were separated, with the guys on the side of the island with thirteen beautiful single women who flaunted themselves in teeny-tiny swimsuits. The girls were subject to similar temptation on their side of the island, where thirteen handsome men attempted to seduce them. Tribal games included sexual innuendoes and intimate touch. It was the season's number one show.

As our Sunday school discussed the show we were asked, "Would you put yourself in that arena of temptation?" The consensus was a resounding no. Of course, it would be ridiculous to place ourselves into such an arena of temptation. But I wonder how many of us could have said no if asked whether we place ourselves in the arena by watching it on TV.

"No, I'd never go to *Temptation Island.*" (At least not physically, just by TV.)

"No, I'd never laugh at sexual unfaithfulness." (Well, OK, just maybe a few "Must-See TV" sexual innuendoes, but that's just humor, right?)

"No, I'd never expose myself to pornography." (No way! Not pictures, but those mental images from my Harlequin stories . . . well, I just skip over them!)

The media deeply affect us. Sometimes . . . tragically. Serial killer Ted Bundy, who was executed for killing several young girls and women, believed so. Twenty-four hours before his execution he said, "What scares me . . . is when I see what's on cable TV . . . some of the movies . . . some of the violence that comes into homes today [is] stuff they wouldn't have shown in X-rated adult theatres 30 years ago. This stuff . . . I'm telling you from personal experience, is the most graphic violence."[3]

That was in 1989. Imagine what he would think today! From that date until 1999,

Foul language was up 550 percent.

Sexual content was up 300 percent.

Gay sex references were up 2,650 percent.[4]

And that's just on cable TV! Step into an R-rated movie, and your senses are likely to be on sexual and violence overload. Do you think you can actually expose yourself to that kind of stuff and still understand the true meaning of sex . . . the pure, passionate tenderness of a holy marriage bed?

My husband and I discovered that we could not expose ourselves to most movies and certain television programs without deeply affecting our marriage. Today we have guidelines to protect us from falling prey to their effects.

Is Your Life Void of Quiet Because of the Chaos of the Culture?

It's not always the content of the media that hurts your marriage, but the clutter and noise it creates in your life. When was the last time:

- You sat in the stillness and quietness of the day for at least thirty minutes?
- You went to bed an hour early just to be with your husband...TV off?
- You sat on a park bench with your husband's head in your lap dreaming about the future?
- You said no to someone's request for your precious time?

Far subtler than the content of our entertainment is the busyness that the media culture creates. Between our forty-hour-plus work weeks, we find rest . . . in front of the television or the big screen.

Let me ask you something. How many deep, meaningful conversations have you had with your husband during the commercial breaks of "Must-See TV"? How much energy do you have to share with him after an at-home video marathon or a late-night flick at the theater?

It's not just the media, either. Social clubs, kids' calendars, and even the church clamor to create a busy clatter in our lives.

Sweet Mother Teresa said in 1977 that "Jesus loved us by giving up His life for us. We too must give ourselves to one another. Because of this, *we must reject whatever would keep us from giving ourselves to one another. We must look at it as something dangerous, something that would destroy us.* I think that anything that destroys or opposes this unity cannot come from God. It comes from the devil (italics added)."

Is there enough quiet in your life? Are you protecting your family's alone time?

Hebrews 4:9–11 says, "There remains, then, a Sabbath-rest for the people of God; for anyone who enters God's rest also rests from his own work . . . Let us, therefore, make every effort to enter that rest, so that no one will fall."

Oh, hey! I just mentioned that whole Sabbath thing in the last chapter and here it is again. (But from the New Testament. Guess it didn't go out with the "law" after all!)

Notice that this verse doesn't say, "When you have a quiet moment, rest." It says *"Make every effort"* to enter that rest. It takes a concentrated effort to rest in our crazy culture. Are you making that effort? Or does that fake pearl of entertainment and acceptance just dangle far too comfortably from your neck? It's not a fashion statement, my friend. It's a noose that often leads to the next fake pearl, and this one is a whopper. The cost of it is just too great a risk. Let's look at a very dangerous fake pearl and call it what it is . . . lust!

It's Your Turn

Invite the Spirit to show you where the clutter of the culture is becoming powerfully oppressive in your life. Don't expect it to be easy to identify. It's not. Pray for God's Spirit to teach you.

"Lord, don't let today's culture snatch truth from my heart. Instead, let me hope in Your Word."

(BASED ON PSALM 119:43)

"God, may I never exchange the truth of God for a lie. If I have done this in the way I entertain myself, please show me."

(BASED ON ROMANS 1:25)

"Search my heart, Lord. I can't identify the junk, but You can. See if there is anything wicked in me, and lead me away from it. Show me if there is anything I am letting into my heart and mind that is offensive, and lead me away from it forever."

(BASED ON PSALM 139:23–24)

"Your Word says that anyone who does not have rule over his own spirit is like a city with broken walls. If I don't protect my marriage by ruling the content in my heart, I can expect it to be broken down. Father, don't let me be deceived, but let me guard my heart."

(BASED ON PROVERBS 25:28)

NOTES:
1. Bob Smithouser, "Mind Over Media," *Focus on the Family Magazine,* April 2001, 7.
2. Jane Hall, "We're Listening, Ted," *Los Angeles Times,* Calendar Section, 3 April 1994.
3. Interview with Dr. James Dobson, Taped January 23, 1989, and shown in *Mind over Media,* Focus on the Family, 2001.
4. *Mind over Media* Discussion guide, Focus on the Family, 2001, Page 2.

"I put this in human terms because you are weak in

your natural selves. Just as you used to offer the parts of

your body in slavery to impurity . . . so now offer them

in slavery to righteousness leading to holiness."

ROMANS 6:19

CHAPTER SEVEN

THE ENEMY'S FAKE PEARLS:
Sexual
Self-Confidence

*I sat there in disbelief. This could **not** be happening to me. He wasn't even attractive. I barely knew him. How was it that my heart was so interested in this man? Here I was "happily" married and yet . . . I was at risk of an emotional affair.*

I reached for the receiver to call my mom. I was going to tell her, and I was not going to give in to this silly whim. I wasn't about to stay in this place.

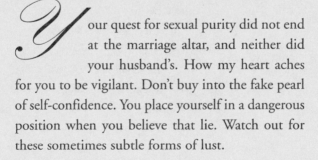

our quest for sexual purity did not end at the marriage altar, and neither did your husband's. How my heart aches for you to be vigilant. Don't buy into the fake pearl of self-confidence. You place yourself in a dangerous position when you believe that lie. Watch out for these sometimes subtle forms of lust.

STORMIE OMARTIAN ON EMOTIONAL AFFAIRS

DANNAH: GIVE US A SNAPSHOT IN YOUR MARRIAGE. TELL US SOMETHING VERY SPECIFIC THAT HAPPENED IN YOUR LIFE. SHOW US A MOMENT WHEN YOU CAN SAY, "I AM PROUD OF MY DECISION TO PROTECT THE PURITY OF MY MARRIAGE."

STORMIE: THERE WAS A TIME WHEN I WAS GOING THROUGH A REALLY HARD STRUGGLE IN MY MARRIAGE. YOU KNOW, ONE OF THOSE TIMES WHEN EVERYTHING IS DYING. YOU JUST FEEL HOPELESS. YOU AREN'T COMMUNICATING WELL. THEN, INTO OUR LIVES COMES THIS MAN THAT MY HUSBAND IS WORKING WITH, AND I FEEL A SUDDEN, STRONG ATTRACTION TO HIM. I WAS SO SHOCKED. IT WAS REALLY STRONG. I THOUGHT, *OH, I AM GOING TO GRIEVE THE HOLY SPIRIT.* NOW, THE MAN NEVER KNEW I FELT THIS, BUT I WAS SO CONCERNED ABOUT IT. I WAS UPSET THAT IT WAS EVEN IN ME. I WENT THAT AFTERNOON INTO MY PRAYER CLOSET AND LAID ON THE FLOOR ON MY FACE AND CRIED AND FASTED AND PRAYED AND SAID, "GOD, I AM NOT LEAVING HERE UNTIL THIS IS BROKEN." I HAD TO CONTINUE IT THROUGH THE NEXT DAY BECAUSE IT WAS SO STRONG.

(continued on page 61 . . .)

Are You in Danger of Emotional Impurity Affecting Your Marriage?

The best of us fall for it. I almost did. So did the author of the best-selling *Power of a Praying Wife*, Stormie Omartian. Check out her righteous response in the sidebar of this chapter.

As for me, I was thankfully and ironically in a place of intimate prayer when I realized I was at risk. Innocent time spent with a male acquaintance had turned into receiving something emotionally that my husband was not giving me. Within twenty-four hours of recognizing it, I told both my Christian counselor and my mom, and we got on our knees together and prayed for protection to surround my marriage. Within a week I found myself laughing at the attraction and wondering where it had come from. Amazing how quickly the Adversary flees when he is exposed. He just can't find the fun in it when his blackmail is useless.

It can happen so easily. Just today, as I was reading proofs of this book, a male acquaintance called whose wife has a medical condition similar to one my husband struggles with. This condition means we sometimes miss fun stuff and have to slow down at the most inconvenient times. This man offered one word of kindness. "How's Bob's health?" Oh, I wanted to open up and tell the past week's disappointments. But the Spirit warned me I could not go into that emotionally intimate place with a man. And I thanked God when I got of the phone.

Ever found yourself in that place where another man is meeting an emotional need that your husband is not? Or do you see your husband spending time with a woman either at work or in other social settings? Are you afraid there is a risk there? You are not alone. But don't let that be an excuse to passively accept it.

Sexual impurity is a zero tolerance arena! You are on shaky ground if there are emotional bonds being created between you and another man (or your husband and another woman). Those bonds begin with little things like:

- Innocently having lunch alone with a man

- Seeking advice from a man about personal issues, especially marital issues

- Seeking or accepting frequent praise or affirmation from the same man

- Being or becoming comfortable with being alone in an office or a home together

Emotional bonds are growing, and you are in danger of the emotional affair becoming physical when:

- You intentionally seek out time to be with this man

(continued from page 60 . . .)

THE FEELING WAS GUT-WRENCHING AS I STAYED THERE WITH MY FACE IN THE CARPET AND KEPT PRAYING, "I CAN DO ALL THINGS THROUGH CHRIST WHO STRENGTHENS ME."

GOD BROKE IT COMPLETELY. IT WAS SO TOTALLY GONE THAT WHEN I LOOKED AT THAT PERSON THE NEXT TIME I THOUGHT, "WHAT *WAS* THAT ALL ABOUT!" I WAS NOT ATTRACTED TO HIM AT ALL. IT WAS A SET-UP BY THE DEVIL BECAUSE MY MARRIAGE WAS STRUGGLING.

DANNAH: I'VE STRUGGLED WITH THAT ONCE TOO. I THINK MOST WOMEN DO, BUT WE DON'T TALK ABOUT IT.

STORMIE: YES, IT'S VERY COMMON. WE'VE JUST GOT TO TALK ABOUT IT AND SAY, "THIS CAN HAPPEN, AND IT IS WRONG." WE CANNOT ALLOW OURSELVES TO BECOME ATTRACTED TO PEOPLE OF THE OPPOSITE SEX. THE MINUTE THAT FEELING HITS YOU, YOU SHOULD BE ON YOUR FACE AND ASKING GOD TO BREAK IT. IT IS SO OF THE DEVIL.

• You manipulate your schedule to see him

• You spend time fantasizing about him.

Do you see some of these characteristics in your friendships with guys? Run for cover—and fast!

Understand that I'm not saying you can't have healthy, innocent friendships with men once you are married . . . but they can't be close friendships. You have to set up strong standards to avoid the temptation of an emotional affair. Have you done that, or are you at risk?

Is Pornography Affecting Your Marriage?

Recently I was at a "meeting of the minds" in a Christian setting where more than ten thousand Christians came together. But, oh, even in that place I was reminded of how far-reaching and threatening is the dark reality of pornography.

In two different meetings with women who work in recognizable positions for high-profile Christian companies, I was met with the horrible ruin of pornography. One woman confided in me that she'd been separated for more than a year with only a small handful of people knowing her pain, due to her position. Her husband continues to operate in denial mode despite the fact that she has found proof of his addiction to pornographic magazines. A once-hopeful pair of two committed Christians now teeter on the edge of divorce. Their separation came after years of counseling and attempting to overcome the distance, lack of intimacy, and horrible emotional turmoil caused by the pornography. She's not sure the marriage will survive the lure of a paper woman.

Another woman told Bob and me that her marriage was in recovery from pornography. Having faced the same distance and lack of intimacy due to pornography largely from the Internet, she finally called for a separation. Her husband valued the marriage more than his lustful addiction and submitted himself to SLAA (Sex and Love Addicts Anonymous) meetings and the pursuit of Christ for the first time. They've been back together now for four years but are still in the long process of living as a family marked by the presence of a "recovering sex addict." She's both encouraged by his honesty and hurt by his confessions when occasionally he loses ground.

Both women shared a common thread as they whispered to us in the midst of that crowded mass gathering. They feel utterly and hopelessly alone. But they are not alone. Focus on the Family's Website recently posted a question "Has pornography ever been a problem in your home?" Forty-six percent of respondents said yes.[1] Pornography is creeping into the strongest of homes. In August of 1999, 20 percent of the calls to Focus on the Family's Pastoral Care Line were from pastors struggling with on-line porn.[2]

If you know pornography is a problem or suspect it's a problem, know that you are not alone. But don't sit by passively dismissing it. Pornography is a chemically addictive destroyer. Dr. Mark Laaser, former pastor and recovering sex addict, says, "Don't underestimate the power of fantasy. Given the chemical changes it creates, sex addicts are, in reality, drug addicts."[3] Side effects for users can include lack of productivity, inability to meet obligations, emotional numbness, social withdrawal, lack of drive for sex within marriage, and more. Slowly but powerfully, pornography becomes an adulterous mistress.

The Promise Keepers movement has done a lot to equip men to discuss their temptation and failures in the area of pornography. In 1996, 21 percent of active and committed Promise Keepers reported that purity was the most difficult of the seven promises to keep.[4] It's time for women, as the other half of the one-flesh relationship, to understand the great risk of pornography preying upon our husbands and to lovingly walk beside them free of our naïveté.

Is Your Marriage Crumbling Because of an Outright Adulterous Affair?

Approximately 40 percent of married men will have an extramarital affair at some time. That figure rises to 70 percent for those making more than $70,000 per year. Thirty-three percent of married women will be involved in an extramarital affair.[5]

The Bible says that "the eyes of man are never satisfied." If that's true . . . and the Bible always is . . . then we are certain to fall prey to temptation at some time. God's Word also says that he who thinks he won't fall is at risk to do just that!

Do you recognize the risk of adultery? If you do, I believe you to be a wise woman. I stand with you. In confident humility, I believe my God will keep my husband and me faithful, but I acknowledge the risk so that I will be vigilant in guarding against it.

To deny that sexual sin can affect your marriage is to invest in the fake pearl of self-confidence. Romans 6:19 says that you are "weak in your natural selves." We live in a sex-saturated culture. In 1998, pornography alone was a $12–13-billion-a-year industry. Even the combined revenues of the Coca-Cola and McDonnell Douglas corporation giants do not compare.[6] Every day we are at risk of becoming prey to the aggressive purposes of those peddling sex. Don't think yourself above it. Call upon the grace of God to protect you and your husband.

If you don't, you can expect to end up where my husband and I did. Investing in the fake pearls of status and stuff, social acceptance, and sexual self-confidence brought us to a place of great risk. On the outside we looked picture-perfect, but on the inside we were falling apart. I'd like to let you see what was happening behind the mask of perfection. We've looked at a few of the impurities that creep into a marriage with the potential of some costly emotional, physical, and spiritual consequences. I know. I invested in these fake pearls and the cost was great. From the outside things looked pretty good but . . . well, how about if I just let you take a peek.

It's Your Turn

Invite the Spirit to show you where there may be cracks in the strength of your marriage's purity. Rewrite these prayers in your journal, and expectantly ask the Lord to reveal those weaknesses to you. Acknowledge that He and only He can keep you from worldly passions. Add to these as God leads you. ▪

"Lord, please do not allow my husband or me to give in to the sinful desires of sexual impurity. Do not allow us to exchange Your truth for a lie. Show me if we have done this at any level."

(BASED ON ROMANS 1:24–25)

"Lord, I admit that my husband and I are weak in our natural abilities. We are at risk of offering parts of our body to the slavery of impurity. I lift both of our bodies up as slaves to righteousness and holiness."

(BASED ON ROMANS 6:19)

"Lord, I know that our hearts are deceitful in all ways. I lift my husband and myself up to You. Do not let us be deceived, but let any sexual strongholds be exposed. Help us to recognize ways in which we have been weakened or deceived in the arena of sexual purity."

(BASED ON JEREMIAH 17:9)

NOTES

1. This information comes from http://family.org, 2/15/01 5:49 P.M., "Hand Count" on-line survey.
2. Christine J. Gardner, "Tangled in the Worst of the Web," *Christianity Today*, 5 March 2001, 44.
3. Laurie Hall, *An Affair of the Mind: One Woman's Courageous Battle to Salvage Her Family from the Devastation of Pornography* (Colorado Springs: Focus on the Family, 1996), 92.
4. *The Promise Keepers* newsletter, vol. 1, no. 4, July/August 1998, 6.
5. Zig Ziglar, *Courtship After Marriage* (Nelson: Nashville, 1990), 60–61.
6. *The Promise Keepers* newsletter, vol. 1, no. 4, July/August 1998, 6.

"What if some did not have faith?

Will their lack of faith nullify

God's faithfulness? Not at all!"

ROMANS 3:3–4A

CHAPTER EIGHT

THE ENEMY'S FAKE PEARLS:

Giving Up &
Starting Over

"It looks like a cottage out of Better Homes & Gardens," commented Donna VanLiere, my close friend from college and now my neighbor.

"Yeah, it kind of does," I said proudly. "All it needs now is a white picket fence!"

We stood looking across the street at my beautiful little home as the painter slapped the last few brushes of the new yellow color onto it. It truly did look perfect.

In the backyard my husband talked on his cell phone while the kids splashed in our own private pool. A row of Bartlett pear trees lined the sideyard like soldiers until they met and surrendered to a magnificent two-hundred-year-old sycamore tree that hovered over the house. Several elaborate flower beds wrapped lazily around the yard.

We'd worked hard to build this life . . . very hard.

We'd also built a little media empire. At the ages of just twenty-six and twenty-seven we owned a full-

service marketing agency, a monthly magazine, and two radio stations. It took up to twenty-six employees to keep it all running smoothly, and we were deeply in debt with multiple bank loans and mortgages. Bob and I each worked several job roles in an attempt to keep costs low and income high.

Together, we had achieved every dream we'd set out to make into reality. We'd even managed to wrap our faith into it all. We were trying to use our corporate adventures to proudly project our faith through contemporary Christian artists being played on our radio station and an entire section in our monthly magazine being devoted to faith issues.

It looked like a perfect life. Weekends we were likely to be found vacationing at the lake with the company Jet Skis.

That . . . or we'd be fighting. Mostly we'd be fighting.

How could it be that we'd worked so hard and found so little fulfillment? I truly wondered if my marriage could make it.

I felt like quitting.

O h, please, please, please . . . don't quit. You don't have to divorce to quit, either. Every day women choose to quit by passively staying in a boring, complacent marriage that lacks passion. Oh, you can wear the mask and just go on in that place of numbness if you want, but the consequences are very similar to divorce. Only your heart might not feel it as much as it grows harder and harder and harder.

I was recently talking with a woman in her thirties who hasn't had sexual relations with her husband for several years. She is sad and lonely. He says he just doesn't need that anymore. Although it is common for all couples to cease sexual relations for some period of time due to stress, sickness, or busyness, it is not natural for it to last so long. I suspected pornography or an affair from the things she was telling me. I encouraged her to go through the tough work of figuring it out. She told me, "It's just really a lot easier to let it stay like it is." She's quitting. She's giving up without the paperwork. Oh, how I wish she would move forward. There are such great promises ahead for those of us who don't quit but who move forward!

Ever hear of the Taj Mahal? Located in India, it's an exquisite tomb of white marble built by Shah Jahan in memory of his wife, Mumtaz. Although it was built in the seventeenth century, it's still one of the most beautiful

ME? DIVORCE? NEVER!

A RECENT STUDY BY BARNA RESEARCH GROUP STATES THAT 27 PERCENT OF BORN-AGAIN CHRISTIANS ARE OR HAVE PREVIOUSLY BEEN DIVORCED. THIS IS IN COMPARISON TO 24 PERCENT OF ALL MARRIED COUPLES.[1] IN OTHER WORDS, THE NOTION THAT BEING IN A CHRISTIAN MARRIAGE MAKES THE CHANCES OF SUCCESS HIGHER IS JUST A PROUD MYTH. WE'RE ACTUALLY AT GREATER RISK, ESPECIALLY IN THE FIRST FEW YEARS OF MARRIAGE WHEN WE'RE MORE LIKELY TO DENY THE RISK.

FIFTY PERCENT OF ALL DIVORCES OCCUR WITHIN THE FIRST THREE YEARS OF MARRIAGE.[2]

EVERY NOW AND THEN, THE ODDS CREEP UP ON YOU AND TAP YOU ON THE SHOULDER, AND YOU SUDDENLY REALIZE IT COULD BE YOU.

DON'T GIVE UP. PLEASE DON'T GIVE UP. WHATEVER ADVICE ANYONE HAS GIVEN YOU, PLEASE HEAR ME: QUITTING WILL ONLY MAKE THINGS WORSE. ■

buildings in existence. It took twenty thousand laborers seventeen years to meticulously carve the lacelike detail into the marble masterpiece and decorate it with ornate, inlaid precious gems and calligraphic messages. It is a monument of one man's love for a woman.

The Shah and Mumtaz could have given up many times on their love. She had to endure more than you and I probably ever will. Prior to her husband's reign as emperor, an attempt was made to kill him. Mumtaz followed him into the hard and miserable life of a fugitive as they hid in caves and forests and in the plains of Bengal with little food and comfort and many children. (She died giving birth to number fourteen.) It looked hopeless. Most of the prince's advisers and friends deserted him. She did not.[3]

Nearly all of us will face our own "plains of Bengal." Your husband's business may fail. He might be fired. You might be. He could become chronically ill. A precious child of yours could face terminal illness. You could face bankruptcy. You could lose your home. Your family may go through a time of shame. Will you stick by your husband like Mumtaz did?

It's never easy to build a pure, passionate marriage. Whether you're just coasting along and ignoring any little impurities—like overworking or speaking unkindly to each other—or whether you're on the brink of giving in because of sexual sin, financial ruin, or a total lack of hope, I want to push

The Emotional Consequences of Quitting

You think it hurts when marriage doesn't feel right? You can't even imagine what it feels like when it ceases to breathe. Frank Minirth, a psychiatrist who has treated thousands for depression, says, "Divorce is second only to death in terms of emotional impact." The pain of divorce is unfathomable.[4]

The Financial Consequences of Quitting

Do you find it tough to make ends meet? Think that without *his* debt you could make it? Think again! The standard of living for women and their children drops significantly following divorce. For every ten dollars you have to spend now, you'll likely have only three to spend after divorce.[5]

The Kids' Consequences of Your Quitting

Do you love your kids? Of course you do! Divorce significantly harms your children. In the midst of your own hurt and recovery, your kids will see either you or their dad infrequently. Usually, it's the dad who takes the hit here. Of course, the kids spend much of their lives trying to fill the void that not seeing their dad creates. They use drugs, anger, alcohol, sex, and violence. They're more likely to struggle with deep emotional problems.

---

you to purify your marriage. Then and only then can you experience the kind of relationship that truly portrays Christ's love.

The journey to purity and holiness is always difficult. God knows we've got to travel the tough road if we are to build the strength to go the distance.

When Pharaoh finally relented and allowed the Israelites to leave their bondage of slavery in Egypt, the Bible tells us that "God did not lead them on the road through the Philistine country, though that was shorter. For God said, 'If they face war, they might change their minds and return to [their bondage].' So God led the people around by the desert road toward the Red Sea" (Exodus 13:17–18).

Imagine that! These poor people had been beaten, enslaved, and worked nearly to death, and when they finally head for freedom, God doesn't let them go on the short road. He takes them the long way! Why? Because He knows they have to go that way or it'd be too easy to turn back when the war rages.

My friend, the road ahead is hard. The war will rage. But take it from one who has traveled it (and is still on it) . . . it is worth it. Are you ready to go the distance? God will stick right beside you. There's an indescribable gift at the end of the road. It's a relationship so fantastic that the Bible calls it a "mystery"! Do you want it? Then please don't quit! Don't quit by getting out of your marriage, and don't quit by giving in to your marriage. Strive with me for something more!

I'd spent the last several months wondering what could fix my marriage. I didn't like to pray about it. When I did, that one thing kept coming up. The one thing I'd decided a long time ago not to talk about.
Surely it couldn't be that. I could never do that! Never!

It's Your Turn

I have a prayer for you today, and I want you to expand upon it in your journal. All of us have moments when we can't really believe God would make our marriage what we hoped. Many of us have moments of great despair. Does that change God's faithfulness to your precious portrait of His love? No! Scripture says not.

Today, start by writing this prayer into your journal and then confess every little area where you've been afraid to believe God could make your marriage better. Give it to Him. He can handle it. You can't!

"Oh God, how I thank You that my own lack of faith will never nullify Your ability to be faithful in my marriage. Even when I am completely faithless, You will remain faithful, for You are faithfulness and You cannot disown Yourself!"

(BASED ON ROMANS 3:3 AND 2 TIMOTHY 2:13)

NOTES

1. www.barna.org, "The Year's Most Intriguing Findings from Barna Research Studies."
   Posted December 12, 2000. Barna Research Online.
   (http://www.barna.org/cgi-bin/PagePressRelease.asp?PressReleaseID=77&Reference=B)
2. Don and Sally Meredith, *Two . . . Becoming One* (Chicago: Moody, 1999), 23.
3. Helen Andelin, *Fascinating Womanhood* (New York: Bantam, 1965), 9.
4. Zig Ziglar, *Courtship After Marriage* (Nashville: Nelson, 1990), 55.
5. Ibid., 53.

"Confess your sins to each other

and pray for each other

so that you may be healed."

JAMES 5:16

CHAPTER NINE

THE ENEMY'S FAKE PEARLS:
Pride & Denial

Tonight I would do what I had put off for ten years. It was time to tell someone. I walked purposefully into the bedroom where Bob was resting.

"I have to tell you something," I said, my words sounding rather rehearsed. And they were. I had been rehearsing since the moment he proposed to me six years ago.

He sat with a puzzled, clueless look on his face.

"This is going to be hard," I warned him. Then we sat in silence.

Maybe I couldn't do this, I thought. Maybe I don't need to do it, I hoped. Maybe it will ruin us, I feared. "I can't look at you," I blurted as I turned out the lights and tears began to fall.

"Dannah!" Bob exclaimed, snapping the lights back on. "What is it?"

As he looked at my face, he began to understand just how hard this was, and his expression changed. He was concerned. He sat back with a new attentiveness about him.

I snapped the lights back off. Silence reigned as the clock's tick marked the thick silence.

The lights snapped on. "Dannah, please tell me," Bob pleaded.

I turned the lights off. "Well, I know you've always thought . . ." I tried to say it, but tears engulfed me. The minutes passed. I composed myself.

"I am so sorry . . ." I tried again.

For nearly three hours we sat there . . . me trying to confess my dark secret . . . him waiting more patiently than he ever had . . . the lights on . . . the lights off.

Finally, as if a battle had been finished, I felt a sense of finality come over me. I took a deep breath. It was time.

"I know you have always thought I was pure, but when I was fifteen I gave myself away," I confessed in a steady tone. The dam broke and emotions took over as I sat there in a ball and cried.

In the darkness I felt a tender hand on my head. A big, warm arm pulled me close. My husband held me. He touched me.

"I forgive you," he said with certainty and grace.

Then he touched me. He really touched me. He didn't miss an inch of my body as he expressed his forgiveness. With each touch I began to feel in my heart what I'd known in my head for so long.

I was forgiven.

Countless women are asking the same question. "Should I tell him?"

I looked and looked for the answer to that question for the first five years of my marriage. I was so sad to rarely find it addressed. I found one book . . . *one* . . . that answered the question, and it told me to be silent. So I was. And the pain wore on . . . until the night of my confession.

As soon as I confessed my sexual sin, healing began. I didn't fully understand this right away. All I knew was that my spiritual life began to blossom, I became emotional again, and the shame was gone. Oh, it took some months and maybe even a couple of years, but the pain from that youthful, sinful relationship began to fade away. Today I can hardly believe it once held such power over me.

I was experiencing James 5:16. That verse encourages us, "Confess your sins to each other and pray for each other so that you may be healed." God's forgiveness is immediate. The moment you ask for it, you receive it. The healing is something that comes more slowly through the nurturing of other Christians as they verbalize God's loving forgiveness.

Some have angrily said to me, "*That* verse is about approaching people you have sinned against for forgiveness. It doesn't apply to confessing past sexual sin to a spouse!" Oh, my friend, after what you've learned about the truth of sexuality, could you fall for such a hollow argument? Can you see that *any* sexual sin is a sin against your husband whether or not you were married to him when you committed it?

I've heard others say, "A sin in the past is covered in the blood, and it doesn't matter anymore." How can you ever be spiritually intimate if there is a spiritual secret locked deeply in the chambers of your heart? How can you be spiritually intimate locking up the testimony of God's forgiveness? Are you so close to sinless that you don't have the joy of a rescue story to tell? And who better to share it with than the man you want most to be spiritually intimate with?

A final big argument is "He might not forgive you, and it could make the marriage worse!" Remember that the purpose of your marriage is to portray Christ's love. How did He show that love? By forgiving us. If you can't risk reaching out for the forgiveness of Christ in your marriage, how will you ever fully comprehend Christ's readiness to forgive?

Of course, there are many situations where a husband is shackled to his own sin or simply is not a Christian and cannot fathom this kind of forgiveness. That is a sad reality. That's why you must always use caution in talking about sexual sin. I would encourage you to seek the opinions of other Christians as to whether or not confessing past sexual sins is appropriate, but make sure they are using a solid, biblical foundation for the opinion they share with you. Bathe your decision to confess in prayer, making sure that this is something you and your husband are ready for. If you see a definite pattern of unforgiveness in him, or you fear he is not spiritually strong enough to hear your confession, I'd suggest talking to an older, wiser woman instead. See if she can walk you through the healing process instead of your husband.

There will be exceptions, but I believe that in most situations, you should tell your husband about past sexual sins. If you tell your sin having first covered it in prayer and then disclosing only the basic fact that you sinned (no details), I suspect you will find new freedom. Men often have their own sexual

ON FORGIVENESS OF SEXUAL SIN

~ BOB GRESH

WHEN DANNAH CONFESSED TO ME, I'D BELIEVED FOR MORE THAN FIVE YEARS THAT SHE'D WAITED FOR ME AS I'D WAITED FOR HER. YET BY GOD'S GRACE THERE WASN'T A MOMENT OF DOUBTING THAT I WOULD FORGIVE HER. SHE WAS STANDING BEFORE ME BROKEN, AFRAID, AND SPIRITUALLY NAKED. HOW COULD I NOT REACH OUT TO HOLD HER? I'VE LEARNED SINCE THEN THAT SEXUAL SIN RIPS A WOMAN'S HEART APART. EVIDENCE OF THIS CAN BE SEEN IN THE FACT THAT SEXUALLY ACTIVE TEENAGE GIRLS ARE SIX TIMES MORE LIKELY TO ATTEMPT SUICIDE THAN THEIR VIRGIN PEERS.[1] THIS EMOTIONAL TURMOIL CAN CREATE SUCH FEAR AND ISOLATION THAT SHE ALLOWS HER SHAME TO MUTE HER DESPITE THE DESIRE TO BE TRUTHFUL WITH THOSE WHO CAN HELP HER HEAL. UNTIL SHE IS COURAGEOUS ENOUGH TO UTTER THE WORDS SHE SO DESPISES, SHE WILL NOT BEGIN TO HEAL. DANNAH AND I HAVE TALKED WITH WOMEN WHO, INSTEAD OF FINDING HEALING, ENDURE FURTHER EMOTIONAL WOUNDS BECAUSE THEIR HUSBANDS WILL NOT FORGIVE THEM.

(continued on page 77 . . .)

baggage in, at the very least, the form of temptation, which gives them a special understanding in this area. Unless you allow your confidence in Christ to override the fear that Satan creates, you will stay locked in a place of spiritual numbness.

Is there something in your life that lingers as a source of shame? Maybe you've hidden a youthful sexual relationship. Perhaps the deep pain of abortion is your secret. Maybe the sexual sin is an affair that has occurred since you've been married. Will you continue to let Satan blackmail you with it, or do you want to experience the healing God has for you?

Let me give you some very important guidelines to follow if you need to approach this tough task.

Pray

You are going on a mission. It's not any easy one. In fact, it can be quite dangerous. The Enemy would love to disrupt the work God is about to do in your marriage. Be thoroughly covered in prayer and Scripture. I've written some prayers based on Scripture just for this situation.

"Lord, You said in Your Word that the old things are dead. Thank You for making a new creature out of me. Help me to feel that. Help me to know that all things are new."

(BASED ON 2 CORINTHIANS 5:17)

"Lord, I reject that conduct of sin, and I pray that You would renew my spirit and my mind, and . . . I accept the new person I am, which was created according to God in true righteousness and holiness."

(BASED ON EPHESIANS 4:22–24)

"Help me to forget past sins, and don't even let me consider them or ponder them. I pray that my husband, too, can release these things and will not hold them in his heart or his mind. I trust You to do a new thing in me and in my marriage as we sever the past. I believe it'll just spring forth in my marriage! I can't wait to know it."

(BASED ON ISAIAH 43:18–19)

2 Determine What You Will Tell

My number one rule is "no mooning!" (Yes, I said "mooning" as in a good old fanny flash!) You never want to use words to create a visual picture of the sin you committed. Your husband should never see in his mind what happened with your body. He should see only what happened in your heart. I've seen many couples robbed of the healing that can occur through confession as they get into graphic details of past sins. Those details are not necessary and shouldn't be told. Period!

If you need to verbalize details because you just can't believe you really are forgiven for something that seems so bad to you, then you need to talk to a Christian counselor who can handle that kind of information in the right way. (I'd recommend a female counselor since the issue is sexual in nature.)

(continued from page 76 . . .)

MEN STRUGGLE DEEPLY WITH SEXUAL TEMPTATION. I'M STILL LOOKING FOR THE MAN WHO DOESN'T STRUGGLE DAILY WITH SEXUAL THOUGHTS. YET SOME OF THOSE SAME MEN CAN'T FORGIVE A WOMAN WHO TODAY LIVES A BEAUTIFUL LIFE OF PURITY BUT ONCE FELL PREY TO THE SAME TEMPTATION HE FACES EVERY DAY. CAN HE NOT SEE THE BEAM IN HIS OWN EYE FOR THE SPECK IN HERS? PERHAPS IT IS THE FACT THAT HE STILL STRUGGLES THAT MAKES IT DIFFICULT FOR HIM TO FORGIVE. JESUS DESCRIBES THIS EXACT SITUATION IN THE PARABLE OF THE DEBTOR. THE DEBTOR IS RELEASED FROM A GREAT DEBT HE OWES THE KING, THEN TURNS AROUND AND THROWS SOMEONE WHO OWES HIM FAR LESS INTO PRISON. HIS REACTION IS A SPIRIT OF ARROGANCE, CONCEIT, AND PRIDE. IT IS THE SAME VILE ACT THAT A MAN DISPLAYS WHEN HE FAILS TO FORGIVE A WOMAN FOR PREMARITAL SEXUAL SIN. GOD HATES THAT PRIDE AND THE SIN IN HIS NATURE.

IF YOU REACH OUT TO CONFESS TO YOUR HUSBAND AND FIND AN UNFORGIVING HEART, LOOK PAST THAT SIN AND SEE THE SINNER—A MAN WHO DOESN'T DESERVE IT BUT DESPERATELY NEEDS YOUR CONTINUED LOVE. ■

If your husband persistently asks for details, I think it is important that you involve a pastor or Christian counselor to work through some of the consequences of this past sin on your marriage. You can work past this curiosity, but please don't feed it by telling details. My experience with countless women is that this is the number one risk in confessing past sexual sin. Details can be detrimental to the healing process. Don't compromise on this. Get godly help.

The extent of my confession to my husband is at the beginning of this chapter. It's all I've told. It's all he needs to know. He's forgiven me so completely that the details do not matter to him. And they shouldn't.

WHAT ABOUT ADULTERY?

CONFESSING PAST SEXUAL SIN WHEN IT WAS WITHIN THE CONFINES OF THE MARRIAGE CAN SEEM FAR MORE DIFFICULT THAN CONFESSING A SIN THAT WAS COMMITTED PRIOR TO THE MARRIAGE. BUT TAKE A CLOSE LOOK. DON'T THE SAME PRINCIPLES APPLY? COVERING IT UP, ESPECIALLY CONSIDERING THE FACT THAT IT COULD COME OUT THROUGH ANOTHER SOURCE ONE DAY, ONLY GIVES POWER TO THE SIN. I DO BELIEVE THAT IT HAS TO BE HANDLED WITH MUCH PRAYER AND GODLY MEDIATION. I WOULD NOT TRY TO CONFESS ADULTERY UNTIL YOU'VE SECURED THE COUNSEL OF A CHRISTIAN TRAINED AND GIFTED WITH HELPING YOU AND YOUR HUSBAND WALK THROUGH THIS PAINFUL HEALING PROCESS CAREFULLY. ▪

3 Consider Inviting an Older, Wiser Woman to Pray for You

If you still feel afraid and need some extra courage, or you are just not sure if your husband is spiritually mature enough to offer you a godly response, consider telling another woman before you tell him. Choose her wisely with much prayer and ask her to help you follow through. Just telling her will promote healing in you and make it easier to talk to your husband.

4 Just Do It

There's never going to be a perfect time. I looked for that perfect time for five years and always found excuses instead. If you've got a secret sin, it is a stronghold in your marriage. Break through it today!

It's Your Turn

If you fall into the category of women who have sexual sin in their past, this entire chapter is an opportunity for you. Go back through it and work through each part of it prayerfully.

If you don't have issues of sexual healing to work through with your husband, then I have a challenge for you. Your mission is to determine guidelines for receiving a confession. You might have a friend who needs you and, sad to say, we girls often struggle with controlling our tongues. Not only is that sin, but it drastically harms the healing process. ▪

Read James 5:19–20 • Colossians 3:12–13

What is our responsibility to our Christian sister when she is found to be in a state of sin?

Read James 1:26 • James 3:7–9 • Psalm 34:13 • Leviticus 19:16

Christians are often quite sly about how they gossip. They say things like, "I need to ask you to pray for . . ." Ouch! What does the Bible say about the power of the tongue? What is God's opinion of the misuse of the tongue? How much do you think the presence of gossip inhibits healing?

Read Proverbs 26:20–22

What effect could "asking for prayer" or "confiding" in people have on the person who has confessed to you?

Read Proverbs 10:19 • Proverbs 11:22

Some people may need to know what your friend is going through. (She may ask for your help in dealing with family members or need you to help her to find a Christian counselor or to confess to her pastor.) What guidelines should be used when you do need to talk to a third party?

NOTES
1. Barth D. Kirby and Fetro Leland, "Reducing the Risk: Impact of a New Curriculum Among Youths in California" (*Family Plan Perspectives*, 1991), 23:253–63.
2. Paraphrase by Bob Gresh.

"For though we live in the world, we do not wage war

as the world does. The weapons we fight with are not

the weapons of the world. On the contrary, they

have divine power to demolish strongholds."

2 CORINTHIANS 10:3–4

CHAPTER TEN

The Pursuit of the Pearl

This must be what it feels like to be a new Christian as an adult, *I thought.*

The forgiveness my husband had extended to me taught me how complete and real is the forgiveness of my Savior. It was the most radical lesson in faith I'd ever experienced. My enthusiasm for the Bible was like never before.

I opened my pen and began journaling my praise to God for the newness—not just in my marriage—but in me.

"Oh, Lord, having been forgiven by You I am ever grateful to enter into Your presence. On a moment-by-moment basis I sense You changing me. Slowly, ever-so-slowly. It is what I have yearned for and now it is here.

"It all started because four weeks ago I got serious about prayer."

For the first time in years, I was really praying. I'd read a book that challenged me to abandon the petty fifteen-minute routine devotional life and enter into an hour-long daily scheduled appointment with the God of the universe. I could remember sitting there the first day at my kitchen table and thinking the hour would never end, but after only four weeks of never missing that appointment, my life was changing.

I was changing.

It was amazing, but the things they say about Christ changing someone . . . I was starting to believe it!

It was happening to me.

ou might notice that I haven't mentioned too many of my husband's struggles with impurity. There's a good reason for that. To purify your marriage, we have to start with you . . . not him!

We have to put down our fleshly tools carefully crafted by none other than . . . woman! Tools like:

- the "silent treatment"
- nagging
- manipulation
- emotionalism
- accusations

These are just more impurities . . . more fake pearls that Satan can use to ruin your marriage. Forget them! They don't work. Put them down, if for no other reason than you want to win the war! They are mere weapons of our flesh, and the Bible says they don't work. Second Corinthians 10:3–4 says, "For though we live in the world, we do not wage war as the world does. The weapons we fight with are not the weapons of the world. On the contrary, they have divine power to demolish strongholds."

Put down those weapons of the flesh and pick up the mighty weapons of God. There are two of them.

Weapon Number One

We find the first one in Ephesians 6 when God presents us with our spiritual armor. In the whole armor of God, there is only one piece that we actually wear that is a weapon. The rest are all for our protection. They're defensive. The one piece clearly identified as a *weapon* is the Sword of the Spirit, which is the Word of God. So, grab your Bible first!

Weapon Number Two

We do have one more weapon for warfare . . . prayer. Right after Ephesians 6:17 where the Scripture tells us that God's Word is a powerful weapon, it says, "And pray in the Spirit on all occasions." Our second weapon is prayer.

When you put these two together, you have what the Bible calls *dunamis,* which means "to be able." The English word *dynamite* comes from the Greek word *dunamis.* Wow! Suddenly, we have dynamite in our hands to blow apart the plan of the Enemy. But wait a minute, how do you use this stuff that the Bible calls dynamite?

When I started to pray, truly pray . . . I had already been praying for years. I had my fifteen-minute devotions pretty consistently, and I was keeping a prayer journal and studying the Bible. But I wasn't really praying at all. Not until I made a few changes that were, for me, very difficult.

1 Establish a Protected Prayer Time

Author Becky Tirabassi challenged me in her book *Let Prayer Change Your Life.* Through it I was convinced that if I prayed for one hour a day, prayer could truly change my life. It did. And very quickly.

It's not that one hour is the special formula to connecting with God, but I think that it takes that much solitude to separate you from the craze of this world so that you can hear God.

I do realize that an hour seems like a lot of time. I didn't think I could do it. At the time I was in the height of my workaholic phase and holding three job titles. There were only two times of the day *remotely* flexible for me to spend an hour with God—lunchtime and bedtime, which was usually between midnight and two in the morning. But I was convinced, and so I started spending what used to be my power lunches at a local park reading, praying, and journaling for one hour each day.

I say that to say this: Don't tell me you can't find the time. I did. You can too!

Got little kids running around your feet from dawn to dusk? Author Anne Ortlund wrote about rising at 2:00 A.M. to spend one hour with God every night during the years that her children were small. She did it. You can, too!

(Right now, there's a little dude on one of my shoulders telling me to write, "Hey, if you don't think you can handle an hour . . . maybe you could do half an hour. Don't kill yourself . . . stretch yourself." I really want to write this because I don't want you to be overwhelmed. There is nothing you can do to make God love you more, and I don't want your time spent all alone with Him to be a burden or a legalistic act of discipline. But on the other shoulder there is a small guy pleading with me to say, "Hey, there aren't any shortcuts! Remember, I warned you that the road we were taking was the one that required toil and sweat! Do you want to know the 'dynamite' power of prayer? Then get out your calendar and start blocking off an hour a day!" There is plenty you can do to love God more, and spending time alone with Him is at the top of the list. Do stretch yourself here, but don't be overwhelmed. I want you to set a good goal for how much time you'll spend with Him and stick to it.

I think I'll let you be the editor of this little section in parentheses. One condition! Pray about it before you start hacking, OK?)

2. Learn to Pray God's Word

I couldn't even imagine the power that would be unleashed when I began, with a focused heart, to pray using God's Word. Watch out! It truly is dynamite! How do you do it?

It's so easy. Here's an example. Proverbs 10:12b says, "Love covers over all wrongs." I'd pray that out loud to my God by saying, "Lord, let there be such love in my marriage that it covers . . . actually hides . . . all the wrong we've done to hurt each other!"

Oh, yes! That's good stuff!

It's Your Turn

Why don't you give it a try?. Open your Bible to these verses and rewrite them as prayers for your marriage.

Psalm 5:3 ....

....

....

....

....

....

....

Psalm 118:8–9 ....

....

....

....

....

....

....

Proverbs 12:4 ....

....

....

....

....

....

....

Matthew 18:18 ....

....

....

....

....

....

....

Romans 3:3–4 ....

....

....

....

....

....

....

3 Record the Power!

It's really tough sometimes to see God at work unless you keep a record of His power in your life. In Bible times people did this by building altars of stone whenever God did something significant in their lives. These altars were to be a testimony to the generations behind them, and they were to give them courage on the days when they felt like they could not see God's hand in their lives.

I like to leave a trail of altars for me to see what God has done in my life. I do this in two ways. *First, I underline and date Scriptures when God makes them powerfully useful in my life.* How I hate to move on to a new Bible when one wears out. The old ones have so many precious altars in them!

Here is an altar I made in my Bible concerning my marriage.

On 11-21-97 I highlighted, underlined, and circled much of Psalm 130. Parts of it read, "If you, O LORD, kept a record of sins, O Lord, who could stand? . . . I wait for the LORD, my soul waits, and in his word I put my hope. . . . Put your hope in the LORD, for with the LORD is unfailing love and with him is full redemption." Beside the last verse I wrote, "It's 100% guaranteed!" His redemption is a sure thing. I was stating my belief in that guarantee when I created that altar.

The second way I make altars is through my prayer journal. Oh, how sweet to look back at my prayers and see how lovingly and completely God has answered them.

On October 10, 1999, I was praying about how my husband was not enjoying his career. He was in the midst of selling his current businesses and was planning to build another one. He'd spent the first ten years of his career building businesses, and he's an enthusiastic and contagious businessman, but I really sensed God calling me to pray for a change. I didn't know when or what. In my prayer journal, on that day, I committed to pray for him "to be in an enjoyable, fulfilling, and successful career that honors God." I wrote Psalm 90:17 beside it in prayer form, saying, "Establish the works of his hands, oh Lord!" I prayed it every day for several months. In the middle of that winter, he came home one day and said, "I think I'd like to make a career change. How would you feel about me applying for the job of Christian school administrator?"

I flipped! (OK, I flipped *out!* Big difference!)

"What? Do you know what they pay?! What on earth would even give you such a desire? We'll never be able to buy a new house." (Could it be that Greed was once again knocking at my door?)

Bob was calm and just explained to me that the school was ready to grow and needed a businessman to administrate the development. He felt it was time for him to stop building his own businesses and start doing God's business.

He asked me to pray about it.

Imagine the kick in the seat of my pants the next morning when I opened up my prayer journal and read, "Establish the work of his hands, oh Lord!"

On May 31, the school board voted to hire him, and I wrote that date in my prayer journal . . . another altar testifying to God's work in our life.

See how this works? Isn't it fun?! I know it may sound like some work. That's because it is. To find the tremendous value in your faith, you have to become a spiritual merchant, which brings me to the Pearl of Great Price. The man who found the Pearl of Great Price in Christ's parable didn't find it accidentally. His life's work was to be a merchant of pearls. We don't really understand that in our day and age. Today culturing makes pearls an easily afforded commodity. But in Christ's day and still today, you'd have to open 15,000 mollusks to find just one natural pearl, and that may or may not be one of great value. Natural pearls were and are quite rare and very valuable. In fact, pearls were so valuable in Christ's day that only real estate was comparable. The merchant who found that Pearl of Great Price probably *did* have to sell everything to buy that pearl. But he didn't find it by accident. He found it because it was his life's business to search for it.

Make it your life's business to search for the treasure God has for you in His Word. Become a spiritual merchant. It'll change your life.

DON'T SAY I DIDN'T WARN YOU! WHEN YOU PRAY FOR YOUR HUSBAND, ESPECIALLY IN THE HOPES OF CHANGING HIM, YOU CAN SURELY EXPECT SOME CHANGES. BUT THE FIRST CHANGES WON'T BE IN *HIM*. THEY'LL BE IN *YOU*. IF THIS MAKES YOU AS MAD AS IT MADE ME, YOU'LL SAY, "WAIT A MINUTE! I'M NOT THE ONE THAT NEEDS CHANGING HERE!" BUT GOD SEES THINGS WE DON'T. HE KNOWS WHERE WE HAVE ROOM FOR IMPROVEMENT. HE DOESN'T HAVE TO SEARCH LONG TO UNCOVER ATTITUDES AND HABITS THAT ARE OUTSIDE HIS PERFECT WILL FOR US.[1]

—STORMIE OMARTIAN

Oh, that's something I should actually warn you about. It'll change you.

In my life, the first few months of prayer were a love affair rekindled, but a strange thing soon started to happen. The closer I got to the holiness of God, the further away I realized I was. I started to see all the junk that I didn't know was there before. I saw how it grieved my God and how it actually was penetrating my own heart. I couldn't have imagined how difficult the next few months would be.

It's Your Turn

Examine your prayer life by drawing a diagram of your connectedness to God from your junior high years through today. Use a simple line graph, raising the line for periods when you were closer to God. Note special events or efforts that coincided with the times when you prayed more. Look for how God has worked in your personal prayer relationship.

Now in your journal write a commitment about how you will rekindle your alone time with God. In this commitment you should include:

- the length of time you'll try to spend with Him every day

- when you'll spend that time

- where you'll spend it

How is this different or similar to what you've done in the past?

NOTE
1. Stormie Omartian, *The Power of a Praying Wife* (Eugene, Oreg.: Harvest House, 1997), 26-27.

"The kingdom of heaven is like a merchant looking for

fine pearls. When he found one of great value, he went

away and sold everything he had and bought it."

MATTHEW 13:45–46

CHAPTER ELEVEN

Finding the Pearl of Great Price

I sat here at *Lions Club Park soaking in the presence of the Lord. My husband had suggested I take two weeks off work. I needed it to just cry and pray and sleep.*

Now that my head was clear, I could absorb God's truth. What I felt Him telling me was not comfortable. I picked up my pen and painfully began to write my confession and intentions to the Lord.

"Oh, Lord:

"Truly all that I have is Yours and deserves to be cared for as if it were the property of a King. (It is!)

"I have allowed my talents to consume who I am and so find myself using them poorly.

"My most precious gifts—my children and my husband—suffer. They come last. Truly. I am not caring for them like the good steward. I could not give them back to You today and tell You that I have made them better.

"Forgive me.

"Truly, sacrifices must be made for me to be in a holy place. My pride must be forfeited, as must the money and the freedom to spend. If peanut butter

sandwiches and well-worn jeans are to replace the business luncheons and professional wardrobe, then let it be."

I closed my journal. Was it the end? Or the beginning?

I knew my life was filled with impurity that wrestled against all of the good things of God. My professional hunger was the biggest enemy of my soul. It was time to quit. I had no idea what my husband would think of this crazy idea. It didn't make any sense, but I could not deny that God was calling me to give it up.

He was a king like no other. Great men trembled in his presence. The banks of the world could not compare to his wealth. His army was mightier than any other.

. . . *and* he was hopelessly in love with a simple maiden.

How could he share this love with her?

He could bring her to the palace and clothe her in royal robes, a crown, and invaluable jewels. She would never resist, but would she love him? Or would she secretly dream of her old life?

He could drive down into the valley to greet her mounted on his royal horse surrounded by his armed escorts and bright banners, but would she love him? Or would she simply subject herself to his position?

There was only one thing that could cross the gulf between them. He would descend. He would renounce the throne. He would give up his wealth and power. He would walk away from his very identity. He would take on the worn cloak of a beggar, and he would simply live among her people, allowing her to choose him as he had chosen her. It would be a costly risk. She was worth the cost.[1]

So loved the Savior of this world when He came amongst us as a babe. He gave up His power and position and His rights and privileges to live amongst us, inviting us to choose. He was so incredibly in love with His bride, the church, that He was willing to give up all that He had . . . all that He knew . . . all that He was. And so, He gave up all to obtain her love.

This is the passion Christ speaks of in Matthew 13:45–46 when He tells one of His simplest parables.

"The kingdom of heaven is like a merchant looking for fine pearls. When he found one·of great value, he went away and sold everything he had and bought it."

He's asking you and me to reciprocate His sacrifice. He's asking us to be willing to leave everything we have and everything we are to choose Him. He's asking us to love Him back. And He's warning us it could be very costly.

Although the gift of salvation is free to you and to me, this short parable says that to really pursue God, to really know God, and to love God may require selling *all* that we have. We are challenged to trade in all of the counterfeit investments of our life to buy the real pearl. Christ says in Luke 14:33 that "any of you who does not give up everything he has cannot be my disciple."

Even something seemingly good can become a fake pearl . . . a counterfeit for the real worth of Christ.

Abraham was called to sacrifice Isaac to demonstrate that he was willing to follow God at any cost. This sweet son he'd awaited for so long could have begun to reign in a place in his heart that belonged only to God. And so God called him to sacrifice Isaac to see whether Isaac or God was more important to Abraham. When God sees that the old man has truly made the sacrifice in his heart, He saves the boy. Could a relationship with a child, a parent, a friend become a fake pearl in your life? You bet.

A life's calling can become a fake pearl too. In John 21:15, the resurrected Christ makes an appearance to seven of His followers. They've been fishing when Jesus invites them ashore to enjoy a meal of freshly cooked fish and bread. Peter is there, and Jesus has a question to ask him.

"Simon son of John, do you truly love me more than *these?*" He probes.

I side with the minority who believe that Jesus is referring to the fish and the beloved passion Peter has for the fishing business when He says "these." [3] Perhaps Peter pulls the fish he's enjoying from his lips and uncomfortably shifts in his seat as he says,

STEVEN CURTIS CHAPMAN ON THE COST OF FOLLOWING CHRIST

DANNAH: ONE OF MY FAVORITE SONGS OF YOURS IS "FOR THE SAKE OF THE CALL." IT TALKS ABOUT THE COST OF FOLLOWING CHRIST. AS I LISTEN TO THE SONG, I WONDER, WHAT INSPIRED YOU TO WRITE IT?

STEVEN: I FOUND MYSELF AT A POINT SPIRITUALLY OF JUST BEING. I WANTED TO GO DEEPER INTO THE PLACE WHERE IT BEGINS TO BECOME A FIRE. I DIDN'T WANT TO GO THROUGH THE MOTIONS. WHAT WOULD THAT COST ME TO REALLY DO THAT? DOES IT ONLY MEAN THAT I DON'T GO TO R-RATED MOVIES, OR DON'T HAVE SEX BEFORE MARRIAGE? WHAT DOES IT MEAN TO BE CALLED A LOVER OF CHRIST? I WAS ASKING GOD TO SHOW ME THE ANSWER TO WHAT THE COST WAS. I REALIZED IT DOES COST SOMETHING; IT COSTS EVERYTHING. WHY WOULD I HOLD PEOPLE'S EXPECTATIONS OF ME . . . LIKE POPULARITY? I AM WILLING TO SACRIFICE THOSE THINGS TO LIVE IN GOD'S WAY. IN REALLY UNDERSTANDING AND BEING WILLING TO PAY THE PRICE, I WROTE THAT SONG. IT'S FUNNY, ON THE HEELS OF "FOR THE SAKE OF THE CALL," I WROTE "THE GREAT ADVENTURE." I REALIZED THAT THIS IS THE REWARD FOR THE COST—WE ENTER INTO THE ADVENTURE THAT OUR LIFE WAS CREATED FOR. [2]

A. W. TOZER ON UNCLEANSED LOVE

ABRAHAM WAS OLD WHEN ISAAC WAS BORN . . . AND THE CHILD BECAME AT ONCE THE DELIGHT AND IDOL OF HIS HEART. IT IS NOT HARD TO UNDERSTAND. THE BABY REPRESENTED EVERYTHING SACRED TO HIS FATHER'S HEART; THE PROMISES OF GOD, THE COVENANTS, THE HOPES OF THE YEARS AND THE LONG MESSIANIC DREAM. AS HE WATCHED HIM GROW FROM BABYHOOD TO YOUNG MANHOOD, THE HEART OF THE OLD MAN WAS KNIT CLOSER AND CLOSER WITH THE LIFE OF HIS SON, TILL AT LAST THE RELATIONSHIP BORDERED ON THE PERILOUS. IT WAS THEN THAT GOD STEPPED IN TO SAVE BOTH FATHER AND SON FROM THE CONSEQUENCES OF AN UNCLEANSED LOVE . . . GOD LET THE SUFFERING OLD MAN GO THROUGH WITH [THE SACRIFICE OF HIS ONLY SON] UP TO THE POINT WHERE HE KNEW THERE WOULD BE NO RETREAT, AND THEN FORBADE HIM TO LAY A HAND UPON THE BOY. TO THE WONDERING PATRIARCH HE NOW SAYS IN EFFECT, "IT'S ALL RIGHT, ABRAHAM. I NEVER INTENDED THAT YOU SHOULD ACTUALLY SLAY THE LAD. I ONLY WANTED TO REMOVE HIM FROM THE TEMPLE OF YOUR HEART THAT I MIGHT REIGN UNCHALLENGED THERE."[5]

—A. W. TOZER

"Yeah, of course I do."

Jesus is not satisfied that Peter has relinquished. He asks him again. "Simon son of John, do you truly love me?"

Perhaps Peter glances back to the bountiful harvest of fish they've just hauled in and struggles with thoughts of who'll take over his business. He again reluctantly says, "Lord, you know that I love you."

One last time, Jesus calls him to relinquish . . . to let go of the good thing that is the enemy of his soul, to relinquish his identity as a fisherman and to become a follower of Christ. The cost is high, but the Savior asks one more time.

"Simon son of John, do you *love* me?" He asks as His eyes softly plead with Peter to love Him back. And Peter does.[4]

Sometimes our fake pearls are even the dreams we had for our marriage. We all long to give ourselves completely to someone. We yearn to belong and to be loved. Proverbs 19:22 says, "What a man desires is unfailing love; better to be poor than a liar." What does that say to you? To me it says, "Admit it. You desire to be loved without fail. It'd be better for you to be dirt poor than to lie about this and pretend it isn't your heart's desire!"

Often in our passion to know unfailing love, we plug into things or people. Many times we struggle with trying to get this unfailing love from our husbands. Guess what? It'll never, ever happen. He may be the greatest lover, have the most romantic heart, and all but worship the ground you walk on; but he'll never be able to give you unfailing love to the level of fulfillment that your heart craves.

The Bible uses the words "unfailing love" thirty-three times. Never does it refer to any-

JESUS AND THE PEARL

ONE OF THE LARGEST PEARLS EVER KNOWN WAS OWNED BY CLEOPATRA, THE LAST RULER OF THE EGYPTIAN EMPIRE. PTOLEMIC DYNASTY HISTORIAN PLINY ESTIMATED THE VALUE OF HER PEARL TO BE 80,000 POUNDS STERLING. HE MADE THAT ESTIMATE SOMETIME PRIOR TO HIS DEATH AT THE FOOT OF POMPEII. IT'S QUITE POSSIBLE THAT JESUS HEARD OF THIS GREAT PEARL DURING THE TIME THAT HIS FAMILY LIVED IN EGYPT, JUST THIRTY TO FORTY YEARS AFTER CLEOPATRA'S DEATH.

one other than God as the source! God alone can provide unfailing love for you.

It's not wrong to desire that love. It's not wrong to think you desperately need it, but don't look for it where it cannot be found. Are you looking to God for unfailing love, or are you trying to get it from your husband?

If Jesus were in the room with you right now and looked through your heart as He did Peter's, could He see something there that you were clinging to? If He were to ask, "Do you love Me more than these?" could you say yes? Would the investment of your time, your money, and your emotional resources portray your desire to pursue the Pearl?

It's Your Turn

Do you love Him? What fake pearls do you cling to? I was clinging to my career and the stuff I had and wanted because there was never enough. My entertainment choices were often fake pearls that disabled my spiritual life, and I was really expecting my husband to be the source of my contentment and unfailing love. Got any of your own? Why not prayerfully write a list of the fake pearls you've been clinging to, and then present that to God along with a commitment to pursue the Pearl of Great Price.

NOTES
1. This is a paraphrase of a story told by Søren Kierkegaard in Philosophical Fragments, and quoted in Philip Yancey, *Disappointment with God.*
2. Reprinted from my earlier book, *And the Bride Wore White* (Chicago: Moody, 1999), 108-109
3. It's widely believed that Jesus was referring to the others in the group when He said, "Do you love me more than these?" But some Bible scholars think He was referring to the fishing business.
4. John 21:15–19.
5. A.W. Tozer, *The Pursuit of God,* (Harrisburg, Pa.: Christian Publishers, 1961), 24, 26.

CHAPTER TWELVE

The Pain of
the Pearl

It had been months since I'd begun getting the junk out of my own life. And it was wonderful. Painful, but wonderful. I'd quit my job, resigned from several community clubs, and was finding time to rest and relax with my family for the first time in a long while. There was just one thing that truly frightened me about the whole thing.

Today I sat pleading with the Lord about it, "Please, God! Don't take me to a place spiritually that You don't also bring my husband. I would rather be separated by oceans than by this great spiritual gulf that I see growing every day."

Even as I uttered the prayer, I felt prompted very clearly to go to the mailbox.

And there it was.

Addressed to my husband.

A nondescript, brown envelope.

Inside were pictures vile enough to make me sick to my stomach. It was a promotional packet. Nothing he'd ordered. But I sensed it didn't arrive by accident.

My husband had struggled with pornography as a teen. My heart had ripped when he told me shortly after we'd married that his curiosity hadn't ceased with our own sexual activity, which he had faithfully waited for. Through the years, he'd been very open with me when the temptation overwhelmed him. Through his own humble confessions, I knew that this was his greatest stronghold.

Each time we had talked about it I had wrestled with the pain that it caused **me***, never considering his own spiritual struggle to stand pure before the God he loved desperately. My usual response was to punish him with silence or an emotional display or to withdrawal from him physically. Today was different. I didn't feel those same selfish emotions. Just sadness. Today my heart broke for him and with him instead of for myself.*

I returned to my Bible in tears.

"God, what should I do?" I pleaded. "What should I do?"

By the end of the afternoon, I had an answer that I felt was from God. I didn't like it.

I returned to my Bible. As I read that day, I felt God telling me that **I** *couldn't do anything. That I was not the source of my husband's ability to stand pure before God. I needed to give my sweet husband room, but the thought of that frightened me very much.*

I spent the afternoon pleading with the Lord to give me a perceptive heart. I went to the local Christian bookstore, just hoping there'd be a book titled, Dannah's Guide to Her Husband's Sin!

*And there it was—*Tough Love *by Dr. James Dobson. Glaring out at me from the end of the display rack. I'd heard of it but never once thought it was for me. Today I knew it was.*

I went home and between tears devoured it in one afternoon.

The book answered my questions and even convinced me that the obvious impurity in my husband's life wasn't the one God most deplored. The same greed for status and things that I'd been suffering from was overwhelming my husband, but that hadn't bothered me before because it always benefited me.

After some time in deep prayer, I knew what I needed to do. I had to stop empowering his own greed, pride, and lust by being passive; and I had to stop fueling his impurities by acting selfishly. Like me, Bob had to feel the holy consequences of his strongholds to be able to come out from under them. I knew just what to do, but I sure didn't want to do it.

Tonight was not the night. I wasn't covered in prayer to do what I knew God wanted me to do.

Besides, I was scared silly.

*W*hen you search for purity by pursuing the Pearl of Great Price, it consumes you. You begin to become like it. As you live a lifestyle of purity—free from the fake pearls this world dangles in front of you every day—impurities become painfully unbearable. Because of the pain, you can't help but adjust your life to get rid of them. God *uses* the pain to work them out of your life much like a pearl is developed out of great pain.

A mollusk begins to develop a natural pearl when it becomes aware of a painful impurity embedded deep within its soft interior. As it detects the impurity, caused often by a grain of sand or a teeny, tiny fish, it begins to notice that it has been exposed to disease. It's then that the little sea creature begins to faithfully cover the point of pain and begins the work of creating a precious pearl.

You may feel the deep pain of your own impurities. Or you may be painfully aware of your husband's impurities. I was, and the point of pain called me to speak out. I just had to be careful *how* I did that.

I'm talking about righteous anger. It is the kind that detects unholiness and feels the pain that causes the anger. This kind of anger is not displayed reactively, but with a kind and holy, compassionate word spoken in boldness. This kind of anger draws a line in the sand and calmly says, "You crossed the line!"

For too many years, I misused anger as a regular practice. I vacillated between passively ignoring my feelings when Bob's sin hurt me and explosively reacting when the hurt bottled up enough. I did this until God began to teach me the power of using anger righteously. I want to suggest to you that using bold speech to lovingly confront unholiness in your marriage is not only OK, but vital. Expressing anger this way is to simply and calmly tell the truth.

"I BELIEVE THAT THE HUMAN CAPACITY FOR ANGER IS ROOTED IN THE NATURE OF GOD. . . . ANGER DERIVES FROM TWO ASPECTS OF GOD'S DIVINE NATURE: GOD'S HOLINESS AND GOD'S LOVE. . . . ANGER IS EVIDENCE THAT WE ARE MADE IN GOD'S IMAGE; IT DEMONSTRATES THAT WE STILL HAVE SOME CONCERN FOR JUSTICE AND RIGHTEOUSNESS IN SPITE OF OUR FALLEN ESTATE."[1]

—GARY CHAPMAN

In Proverbs 23:23 we are encouraged to "buy the truth and do not sell it." Every day we women sell the truth. We sell it because we aren't willing to endure the thought of "what people might think." We sell it because it will cost time and maybe money to receive the wise counsel we need to make our marriages healthier. We sell it because it may cost us a period of distance in our marriages when we have to cling to our faith and not our husbands. We sell the truth and then live the lie of a "picture-perfect marriage" so no one will see the hurt.

Don't do that. Don't sell the truth. Righteously speak it into your marriage and claim the promise of Proverbs 12:19, "Truth stands the test of time; lies are soon exposed" (NLT). Know that there is power in a holy word spoken with boldness. Proverbs 9:8b encourages us by saying, "Rebuke a wise man and he will love you."

FOUR LEVELS OF SPEAKING THE TRUTH IN LOVE

I THINK THERE ARE FOUR LEVELS OF SPEAKING THE TRUTH IN LOVE. AT EACH LEVEL WE ARE APPROPRIATELY DRAWING A LINE OF BEHAVIORAL EXPECTATIONS TO PROTECT OUR MARRIAGE. TO BE EFFECTIVE, THIS HAS TO BE DONE WITH CONTROLLED, LOVING SPEECH.

LEVEL 1   SPEAKING THE TRUTH THROUGH DAILY CONTROLLED BOLDNESS

WE'VE GOT TO BECOME MASTERS OF JAMES 1:19, WHICH SAYS, "EVERYONE SHOULD BE QUICK TO LISTEN, SLOW TO SPEAK AND SLOW TO BECOME ANGRY." MEMORIZE THAT VERSE AND EXEMPLIFY IT. THEN YOUR "NAGGING" WILL TURN INTO CONSTRUCTIVE BOLD SPEECH THAT YOU CAN USE TO BUILD THE MARRIAGE RATHER THAN UNCONTROLLED ANGRY SPEECH THAT RIPS IT APART.

FOR EXAMPLE, "I FEEL MORE OPEN TO YOUR CONSTRUCTIVE IDEAS ABOUT HOW I TAKE CARE OF THE HOUSE WHEN YOU'VE TAKEN TIME TO BUILD ME UP WITH WORDS OF ENCOURAGEMENT ABOUT WHAT I AM DOING WELL." OR "IT HURTS ME THAT YOU WORKED LATE AGAIN TONIGHT WHEN YOU PROMISED ME LAST NIGHT THAT YOU WOULDN'T. I LIKE BEING WITH YOU AND HOPE YOU'LL COME HOME ON TIME TOMORROW."

SPEAKING THE TRUTH THROUGH CONFRONTATION WITH A COUNSELOR OR PASTOR

IF THE STRATEGIES YOU'RE TRYING JUST AREN'T MAKING A DIFFERENCE IN YOUR MARRIAGE, IT'S TIME TO TALK WITH A CHRISTIAN WHO'S TRAINED TO GUIDE YOUR CONVERSATIONS. THE OTHER PARTY MAY HELP YOU PINPOINT ISSUES THAT YOU DIDN'T KNOW WERE PRESENT LIKE PORNOGRAPHY, WORKAHOLISM, OR UNFORGIVENESS. IN THIS SETTING YOU CAN CONTINUE THE PRINCIPLE OF USING CONTROLLED BOLD SPEECH.

FOR EXAMPLE, "I FEEL VERY THREATENED BY THE AMOUNT OF TIME YOUR CAREER TAKES FROM OUR FAMILY LIFE." OR "I AM NOT WILLING TO ALLOW PORNOGRAPHY TO BE A PART OF OUR MARRIAGE. I'M HERE BECAUSE I BELIEVE WE BOTH NEED HELP IN HOW TO DEAL WITH IT IN A HEALTHY, HOLY MANNER. TOGETHER WE CAN MAKE IT THROUGH THIS."

SPEAKING THE TRUTH WITH A TIME-OUT

A TIME-OUT REQUIRES THAT YOU LEAVE THE BUSYNESS OF HOME, WORK, AND SOCIAL RESPONSIBILITIES TO TRULY FOCUS ON THE MARRIAGE. IT IS A SHORT TIME THAT CAN BE SPENT TOGETHER OR APART AS LONG AS BOTH MARRIAGE PARTNERS ARE CONNECTED THROUGH THE MEDIATION OF A COUNSELOR OR PASTOR. MARRIED PARTNERS TAKING A TIME-OUT ASSUME THAT WHAT IS MOST HARMING THE MARRIAGE IS NOT ONE MEMBER OF THE MARRIAGE BUT THE BUSYNESS, DISTRACTIONS, AND PROBLEMS OF EVERYDAY LIFE. THEY ARE BOTH WILLING TO MAKE SACRIFICES IN WORK, FINANCES, STATUS, ETC., TO CREATE A PERIOD OF A WEEKEND TO A MONTH TO FOCUS ON THE MARRIAGE.

FOR EXAMPLE, "THIS BUSYNESS IS NOT ALLOWING US TO FOCUS ON THE PROBLEMS IN OUR MARRIAGE, SO I'M ASKING YOU TO TAKE A LONG WEEKEND OFF WITH ME SO THAT WE CAN FOCUS ON US. WE CAN DO THIS TOGETHER, OR I CAN DO IT WITHOUT YOU. EITHER WAY, I'M GETTING AWAY FROM THE PACE OF EVERYTHING TO THINK AND PRAY ABOUT OUR MAR-RIAGE." OR "WE'VE TRIED A LOT OF THINGS AND STILL WE'RE OVERWHELMED BY HURTFUL WORDS; I THINK WE NEED TO TAKE A TIME-OUT FROM EACH OTHER, SO I'LL BE SPENDING THE WEEK AWAY FROM HOME. I HOPE YOU'LL TAKE THIS TIME TO THINK AND PRAY LIKE I WILL BE DOING."

 **SPEAKING THE TRUTH THROUGH SEPARATION**

A SEPARATION IS A DRASTIC STEP. IT SHOULD BE ONLY USED IN THOSE MARRIAGES IN WHICH ADDICTION, ABUSE, OR ADULTERY HAVE BEEN ISSUES. THIS IS TOUGH LOVE AS DESCRIBED IN DR. DOBSON'S BOOK TITLED THE SAME. IT IS OFTEN A LONGER PERIOD OF TIME AWAY FROM EACH OTHER. IF YOU CALL FOR A SEPARATION, YOU ASSUME THAT THE THING DOING THE MOST HARM TO THE MARRIAGE IS THE SIN OF YOUR HUSBAND. IN THE CASE OF A SEPARATION, WORK PATTERNS AND SO FORTH ARE USUALLY CONTINUED BECAUSE THE TIME PERIOD OF THE SEPARATION IS INDEFINITE. THE GOAL SHOULD STILL BE TO HEAL THE MARRIAGE, AND THERE MUST BE A MEDIATING PARTY.

FOR EXAMPLE, "*I LOVE YOU AND CANNOT BE A PART OF EMPOWERING YOU TO CONTINUE HURTING YOURSELF AND THIS MARRIAGE WITH YOUR ALCOHOLISM. I AM HERE FOR YOU WHEN YOU CHOOSE TO TAKE THE STEPS NEEDED TO STOP THIS HARMFUL BEHAVIOR. UNTIL THEN, I WILL NOT BE STAYING IN THE HOUSE.*" *OR* "*THIS ADULTERY HAS HURT ME MORE THAN ANYTHING EVER HAS. I NEED TIME AWAY FROM YOU SO THAT I DON'T HURT YOU WITH MY RESPONSE AND SO THAT YOU CAN THINK ABOUT THE CONSEQUENCES THIS WILL HAVE ON US, THE CHILDREN, AND OTHERS INVOLVED.*" ■

Speaking the Truth Against Divorce-Worthy Sins

Sometimes a woman clearly needs to speak the truth because she is in a horrible, sinful situation. Zig Ziglar writes about such a marriage. The wife was enduring severe beatings at the hand of her high-profile physician husband. The beatings were always followed by tearful promises and pleadings. The wife always accepted his apologies, and the abuse continued until . . .

"One morning . . . her husband awoke from his drunken stupor to see her quietly seated in a chair across from the couch where he had passed out. He . . . started with his usual apologies, explanations, pleadings, and tears. She quietly listened, and after about twenty minutes, she calmly said, "I accept your apologies and understand that you really do love me and that you really didn't know what you were doing. I believe you when you say that you will never hit me again. However, let me tell you what I have been doing this morning. I just got back from a professional photographer's studio. He has taken pictures of every part of my body that has a bruise. I have the negatives that are in safekeeping. I've made arrangements so that if anything happens to me, those negatives and the detailed statement of what has been happening all these years will be turned over to the police.

"After I finished that assignment, I went by the office and made a copy of all of your patients. Just to make sure you don't forget your promise to never beat me again, let me share with you what I will do if you 'forget.' First, I'll send copies of the pictures I just had made to all our friends and social contacts as well as the medical society. Next, I'll send the pictures and a cover letter to all your patients."[2]

The man never beat his wife again. In fact, they went to counseling and their marriage became not only bearable but enjoyable.

I hope you aren't in a situation where abuse, addiction, or adultery is involved. How painful! If you are in that place, you have a righteous reason to boldly confront your husband with the truth in love. Seek out a wise counselor today to begin that process.

If you aren't in that place, thanks for sticking with me because you probably have friends who are or will be in that place. They'll need your advice and love. But let it be a wake-up call to us all. The big impurities don't just show up overnight. They start out as little foxes, and we let them grow right in our own private vineyard.

Speaking the Truth Against the Little Foxes

During my interview with the *700 Club's* Lisa Ryan, she pointed out to me that Song of Songs 2:15 encourages us to get the *little* junk out of our marriage. It says, "Catch for us the foxes, the little foxes that ruin the vineyards, our vineyards that are in bloom."

The "vineyard" represents the love relationship between Solomon and his bride. Note that it is "in bloom" and *still* they are concerned about threats to their love. The "little foxes" represent any kinds of problems that can destroy a relationship. Do you have or have you had any of these little foxes in your marriage? I'll list a few and give you some room to add your own:

- [ ] Busyness
- [ ] Other people striving for your time and affection
- [ ] Hunger for titles
- [ ] Casual and flippant attitudes about having friends of the opposite sex
- [ ] A passion to have a house (a nicer house, a nicer car)
- [ ] A shop-till-you-drop mentality
- [ ] A competitive spirit
- [ ] A "what have *you* done?" attitude about housework

....

....

....

....

....

The little foxes grow when they are fed. Have you noticed any of these things in your marriage? Again, I'll leave some room for you to add your own big foxes:

- [ ] An emotional attachment to someone of the opposite sex
- [ ] An occasional preoccupation with pornography
- [ ] A huge mountain of debt that shackles you to busyness

....

....

....

....

....

I did not have a husband who was beating me or sneaking around committing adultery. I *did* have a husband who really wanted to please me and be close to me, but we were failing miserably. I had a husband who wanted to be a spiritual leader and who loved the Lord, but who had unwittingly released a few "little foxes" into our "vineyard." God's Spirit was telling me that the little things make way for the bigger things. I sensed that the growing distance caused by hurtful words, ignoring each other, pursuing stuff and titles, and exposing ourselves to things opposed to God's holiness were feeding these little foxes.

We'd both tried a half-dozen communication techniques. We'd been to a handful of marriage seminars. Nothing lasted for long. There were simply too many "little" impurities in our marriage for that stuff to work. I was not willing to wait for things to get worse to make them better.

So, I spoke the truth boldly and lovingly. We'd already used kind, confrontational counseling; and he'd even tried hard to make that work, but we were only growing further apart. I wanted to build a passionate, holy marriage and wasn't going to settle passively for anything less. Sexual temptation would *not* be the master of our marriage's spiritual climate. The "mistress" of corporate success would *not* lie in my marriage bed. I *never* said the word *divorce*. I never intended to leave him, but it was time to lovingly and boldly say, "You've crossed the safe boundaries of our marriage, and I'm serious about not letting that happen again."

I felt so utterly alone. I couldn't imagine another marriage in our church being so encrusted with sin . . . so marked by failure. I know now that I was not alone. Approximately 64 percent of Christian men struggle with sexual *addiction* or *compulsion,* which might include pornography, compulsive masturbation, or other secret sexual activities.[3] At one Promise Keepers event, half of the men present said they'd viewed pornography in the week preceding the event.[4] Does this sound hard to believe? Oh, please don't be naive! Pornography is deeply affecting our church, and the problem is growing at a rapid rate. If we want to fight the effects of pornography in our own marriages, in the marriages of our dear friends, and in the marriages within our church, we must first wake up and realize how significant and common the threat is to us.

Given the statistics on the sin of pornography, I'd hate to see the numbers of men struggling with the pursuit of this world's trophies such as titles, salaries, and stuff. This is ever more common. I can tell you that most American men work an average of forty-nine hours each week.[5] Some say they want to work fewer hours but can't afford it. The competitive standards to have material things such as houses, boats, and nice cars and clothes force salaries to be high. Careers and the things they buy pave the way for a lifeless, dull marriage. That's not something I'm willing to settle for. Are you?

How do you know if you are ready to lovingly speak the truth to your husband? And at what level should you address him? Check out the sidebar below. It'll help you to make a decision concerning major confrontations, but I believe a key factor—whether you're just asking him to help around the house more or confronting him with an issue that is really hurting you—is timing. Waiting for that perfect moment—when your heart is pure and his heart is open—is a good idea. Look at the grace of Esther as she prepared to speak the truth.

She didn't run after the king and nag saying, "Hey, your hoodlum friend is up to no good again. I won't have him in my house." (Neither did she silently stand by!)

First, she *fasted!* (She got her own junk cleaned up prayerfully and asked for God to be in her speech.)

Then, she waited for the *right moment.* (It wasn't when she first approached the king that day, or when she made a special dinner that night, but the third time she was with him after she'd decided to present him with delicate information!)

Oh, and she had a wise adviser—her cousin Mordecai. She knew she needed wisdom if her bold speech was going to be effective.

It may seem that confronting is an unforgiving thing to do. On the contrary, I believe that drawing a line in the sand is the first step in true forgiveness. I'd like you to see how boldly confronting my husband and pursuing what for us was a Time-Out turned out to be the catalyst to forgiveness.

SHOULD I TAKE A *TIME-OUT* OR MOVE TOWARD *SEPARATION?*

PROBABLY NOT. THOSE MIGHT SEEM LIKE FUNNY WORDS FROM A WOMAN WHO TRIED A TIME-OUT AND HAD IT WORK. BUT MOST OF THE TIMES WE HAVEN'T *EXHAUSTED* THE POSSIBILITIES OF SPEAKING THE TRUTH IN LOVE AT HOME ON A DAILY BASIS OR KINDLY CONFRONTING UNDER THE WISE MEDIATION OF A PASTOR OR COUNSELOR. HOW DO YOU KNOW IF YOU ARE READY TO MOVE TO A MORE DRASTIC LEVEL OF SPEAKING THE TRUTH? HERE ARE A FEW QUESTIONS YOU NEED TO ANSWER.

1. Have I Tried Levels One and Two?

If you have consistently and lovingly attempted to speak the truth on a daily basis and to use the mediation of a pastor or counselor, then you may consider levels 3 or 4.

2. Does My Husband's Behavior Merit Such a Drastic Confrontation?

If he is actively and aggressively pursuing counseling with you, you probably have no need for a more drastic confrontation. Unless the problems are abusive, addictive, or sexual in nature, it is rarely appropriate to proceed beyond level two.

3. What Is My Motivation?

If your motivation is purely to lovingly build a better marriage, then you *may* be OK to move on to a new level of confrontation. If you have any inkling of motivation to hurt your husband or to put him in his place . . . hold your tongue!

4. Have I Secured the Permission and Assistance of a Mediator?

Do you have a pastor or a counselor with whom you have talked this through and who has helped you to test your motives? We often cannot trust our own motivation in such a situation, and we have to rely upon a unbiased adviser. Ask the person if he or she would be willing to stay in daily contact with you and your husband until you have reached a conclusion to the time-out or separation. If you don't have a mediator, don't proceed.

5. How Long Will This Time-Out or Separation Last?

A time-out should be brief, considering that you should be taking a respite from careers and social responsibilities, and hopefully you can even be away from the responsibilities of your home.

A long weekend or a week is probably a good time to set aside for such exclusive attention to your marriage, but if you can stretch that timetable, by all means go for it.

A separation is a drastic step that must be taken *only* with the advice of a counselor or pastor who will maintain contact with both of you. I don't think that the time frame of a separation should be determined by you, but perhaps by your counselor or pastor.

GARY CHAPMAN
(AUTHOR OF *THE FIVE LOVE LANGUAGES*)
ON SEPARATION

DANNAH: IS IT EVER APPROPRIATE FOR A COUPLE TO CONSIDER SEPARATION THAT IS MONITORED BY WISE COUNSEL?

GARY: I THINK IT CAN BE. ESPECIALLY IN CASES WHERE THERE IS PHYSICAL ABUSE OR EXTREME VERBAL ABUSE OR ALCOHOLISM OR DRUG ABUSE. IN THOSE SITUATIONS, IF SOMETHING IS NOT DONE TO STOP THAT PATTERN, THE MARRIAGE IS NOT GOING TO SURVIVE. SO AS AN ACT OF LOVE THE WIFE SAYS TO THE HUSBAND, "I LOVE YOU TOO MUCH TO SIT HERE AND LET YOU DESTROY ME AND YOURSELF AND CONSEQUENTLY THE NEXT TIME YOU COME HOME DRUNK . . . OR THE NEXT TIME YOU HIT ME . . . I WILL WALK OUT THE DOOR AND BE GONE FOR THREE DAYS." I THINK A TEMPORARY SEPARATION CAN BE HEALTHY. BUT IF IT IS GOING TO BE LOVE IT HAS TO BE SEEN AS THAT. IT IS NOT ABANDONMENT. THE MOTIVATION IS, "I WANT TO BE AN AGENT OF LOVE." AGAIN, IT'S NOT DIVORCE. IT'S NOT EVEN THINKING DIVORCE. IT'S MOTIVATED BY LOVE. THIS SHOULD COME AFTER A PERSON HAS TRIED SOFT LOVE OVER A PERIOD OF TIME. THERE SHOULD BE A GENUINE ATTEMPT AT SOFT LOVE BEFORE TOUGH LOVE EVER ENTERS THE PICTURE. ■

Today was the day I had dreaded. I'd approached two pastors and my Christian counselor. When I told them my story and the plan, each one had said the same thing. "Dannah, if this is of God, you can be confident, but if it is of your own flesh . . . woe be to you!"

My counselor had helped me to establish a time line and was willing to be in daily contact with Bob and me. Her accountability was both a security blanket and a rod to keep us in check.

I walked into the living room to find Bob sitting in the recliner. We were supposed to leave for a family vacation in a few days and he was sitting there looking at the travel brochures. I kneeled down before him and leaned into his lap.

"Hi," I whispered.

"Hey," he grunted. That's just how he was these days. Grumbling, miserable, nonpresent. It wasn't just the junk I found in the mail. It was the debt, the drive for success, the craving of stuff . . . all the same things I'd come to recognize in my own life and was trying to work out. He just didn't see it. Not yet, but I was trusting God to show him.

"I love you," I said confidently and gently.

He looked curiously at me with a raised eyebrow.

"Bob, there's sin in our marriage that I consider to be a huge threat. I know how badly it hurts you and how much you want to get rid of it, so I'm going to do the most loving thing I know to do." I spoke gently

without breaking down as I had suspected I would.

He just listened, seeming to stare right through me.

"I've cancelled our family vacation. We can't afford it, and we're foolish to think we can. We're just using it as an escape from everything else, when all it really does is numb us for a time and build up more debt. Instead, I am taking the kids and going to my parents' house in Pennsylvania so you have some time alone to think," I continued at a steady pace. His eyes grew dark.

"I really do love you," I said as I began to lose composure.

I stood and walked to the front porch and sat on the swing with a hollow feeling.

After a long wait, he followed me.

"I don't deserve this," he retaliated. His eyes were cold and steely and full of hatred.

I wanted to scream, "I take it back! Let's just leave everything like it is. This is too hard. I'm too scared. I don't want to lose you!"

But the Spirit kept me silent and strong. I was holding on to the promise that marriage was something more than this passive live-in relationship.

He turned and began to walk down the street. His hands were in his pocket. His head was hanging low. He looked so lost.

It was the last picture I would have of him before I left.

BOB GRESH ON CONFRONTING IMPURITIES

I BELIEVE THAT MOST MEN FACING PORNOGRAPHY ULTIMATELY KNOW THAT THERE HAS TO BE A TIME WHEN THE LINE IS DRAWN IN THE SAND. THEY NEED TO KNOW THAT IF THEY CROSS THE LINE, THE CONSEQUENCES WILL BE HORRENDOUS. WHEN I WAS INSIDE THE DEPTHS OF MY PROBLEM, I WAS CONSTANTLY DRAWING THAT LINE FOR MYSELF AND FAILING MISERABLY. EACH TIME I'D REDRAW THE LINE, LEAVING MYSELF JUST A LITTLE MORE ROOM FOR SIN.

THE DAY THAT DANNAH DREW THE LINE IN THE SAND, SHE WAS SAYING, "YOU WILL NOT CROSS THIS LINE AND STILL ENJOY THE BENEFITS OF THE FAMILY AND RELATIONSHIP." SHE WAS ULTIMATELY CREATING AND DEFENDING THE "SAFE PLACE" IN OUR HOME. IT'S IMPORTANT TO ESTABLISH YOUR SAFE PLACE.

THE EVENT THAT TRANSFORMED OUR MARRIAGE WAS THE MOMENT THAT DANNAH DEFINED THE BOUNDARIES AND CLEARLY ARTICULATED THAT I WAS ON THE WRONG SIDE OF THOSE BOUNDARIES. GOD'S GRACE KNOWS NO LIMITS. HIS FORGIVENESS KNOWS NO END. BUT HE REQUIRES TRUTH IN THE INMOST PARTS. HE HAS NO PATIENCE WITH SUPERFICIALITY. TURN HARD WHEN YOU TURN BACK TO GOD. ANYTHING LESS IS JOURNEYING IN CIRCLES.

It's Your Turn

Write these verses into prayers for your husband and for you. These are verses that you can use to have discernment in your marriage . . . to see the little foxes and to give you courage to face them. ▪

Proverbs 28:13 ....

....

....

....

....

....

....

....

Psalm 139:23–24 ....

....

....

....

....

....

....

Jeremiah 7:23 ....

....

....

....

....

....

....

2 Peter 1:6–7...

....

....

....

....

....

....

NOTES
1. Gary Chapman, *The Other Side of Love: Handling Anger in a Godly Way* (Chicago: Moody Press, 1999), 19, 23.
2. Zig Ziglar, *Courtship After Marriage* (Nashville: Nelson, 1990), 66.
3. Patrick A. Means, *Men's Secret Wars* (Grand Rapids: Revell, 1996), 132–33.
4. Laurie Hall, *An Affair of the Mind: One Woman's Courageous Battle to Salvage Her Family from the Destruction of Pornography* (Colorado Springs: Focus on the Family, 1996), 236.
5. James T. Bond, Ellen Galinsky, Jennifer Swansberg, *The 1997 National Study of the Changing Workforce* (New York: Families and Workforce Institute), 168.

"I can do all things through

Christ who strengthens me."

PHILIPPIANS 4:13 NKJV

CHAPTER THIRTEEN

Paying the Price of the Pearl

It had been two weeks since I'd driven through the long, rainy night to my parents' home.

Two weeks of waiting.

Two weeks of not wanting to get out of bed.

Two weeks of crying and searching for answers.

Two weeks of pleading with God to work in Bob's life.

Through a phone call from my counselor, he had requested that I return home. He'd requested to see me within the next twenty-four hours because he was ready to participate in our "time-out." He'd discovered a Christian counseling center in Dallas that would take him in. He wasn't taking this lightly anymore. He was going to take three weeks away from the pace of work to pray, think, read, and get advice. He wanted me to come home before he left.

Of course, I said I would. This was a miracle. My success-driven husband was actually leaving his business for three whole weeks!

Here I was the night before I'd see him. I'd imagined this time of separation to be a time when God searched Bob's heart. Instead, He had searched mine. In it, I saw *a thick, black crust of unforgiveness. God was challenging me, and what could I do but rise to it, though I didn't really want to. I pulled out my journal:*

> *"Oh Jesus,*
>
> *"I long for my husband to understand the rip he has crafted in my heart. I yearn to hear him humbly request my forgiveness for giving to others in sin what is rightfully mine. I hope one day he will understand, but today I must prepare myself to be his intercessor to make the pathway to that wonderful day. Today I must forgive him though he does not even understand he needs to be forgiven. . . ."*

I began to list explicitly every way my husband had ever hurt me and all my sins of unforgiveness. I didn't miss a thing . . . from the pornography to the love affair he was having with his career to the debt he'd helped me create to leftover affection he occasionally threw at me. I matter-of-factly wrote and then verbalized each willful act of forgiveness.

And I meant it.

It felt unbelievably freeing.

I just wondered how many months or years I'd have to wait to hear my husband receive that forgiveness.

The merchant who found the pearl of great price paid off a great debt to purchase his treasure. The price was so great that he had to sell everything he had to buy it.

The Pearl of Great Price paid off a great debt to offer you and me the free gift of salvation. The price was so great that He had to give up all He had to pay the debt of our sin.

Your marriage will require you to continually pay off many debts. The price will be great and at times will seem unbearable. The price is often forgiveness.

Forgiveness is costly. Perhaps that's why it is so difficult to model. Instead, we see a lot of unforgiveness in action. Unforgiveness isn't just a spiritual presence. It manifests itself physically. We see it every day.

Gossip is unforgiveness in action.

Passively giving up is unforgiveness in action.

Divorce is unforgiveness in action.

Perhaps forgiveness is so hard to model because we are often fed the lie that forgiveness is a passive, submissive act of overlooking an offense. When forgiveness is approached with this attitude, it is not helpful but hurtful. And it is not an accurate mirroring of Christ's forgiveness. Forgiveness is not a passive act of self-denial but a decisive and protective act of love. Let's look at the truth of forgiveness.

Forgiveness Confidently Acknowledges That a Debt Has Been Created

The Greek word translated *forgive* means "to release from an obligation." If you are going to release someone from an obligation or debt, you must first acknowledge that it exists.

Forgiveness really starts when you draw that line in the sand and calmly say, "You crossed it!" It pointedly marks the debt.

In the Old Testament, Joseph models forgiveness magnificently. Make no mistake how horrid the crime was that was committed against him. He'd been roughed up and left in a dark pit. (Imagine your siblings taking you into an alley and throwing you into a dumpster and taunting you all night long.) He's saved from death. (Imagine listening to them talk of how they will kill you.) But then he's sold into a life of slavery where he'll never hear his father's voice. Instead he'll spend much of it toiling and sweating for someone he doesn't know and much of it in jail because he'll be wrongly accused of crime. (Place yourself in the place of such tremendous emotional turmoil. Imagine the nights you'd sit on a hard, cold cell floor listening to the local drunk ridicule a nearby street gang. You're trying to shut it out by dreaming of your warm bed from which you could hear your mother and father talking.) Eventually, Joseph's brothers show up, and it is time to forgive them for that atrocious act. The first words from Joseph's lips mark the debt his brothers have created: "Do not be distressed and do not be angry with yourselves for selling me here" (Genesis 45:5). He draws the line in the sand and states their sin. Later in his life he will say the famous line, "You intended to harm me, but God intended it for good" (Genesis 50:20). He makes no bones about it. He calls sin what it is.

Forgiveness calmly acknowledges the truth of the debt that's been created.

"You've been unfaithful to me, and I could divorce you."

"You've neglected this marriage, and our children don't feel close to you."

"You've worshiped your career and your paycheck, and I feel no emotion anymore."

Forgiveness doesn't mean you roll over and act like a doormat. Forgiveness boldly acknowledges that a debt has been created.

Forgiveness Doesn't Erase the Practical Responsibility of the Debt

Ask Debbie Morris about forgiveness. She was faced with forgiving Robert Willie who, along with a fellow criminal, raped her when she was just sixteen. That same night they beat and shot her date at point-blank range. The years that followed were years of intense hurt until she forgave Robert Willie. She explains that the forgiveness brought great healing and a sense of release, but it did not absolve Robert Willie of his responsibility for what he did. He was still executed.[2]

A marriage that is hurt—no matter if it is by an adulterous affair or through gradual neglect—will take years to rebuild. There's a great amount of responsibility that one or both spouses must rise up to own. It might cost much pride, money, and time to heal the marriage. That debt is not erased by the verbalization of forgiveness.

This is where forgiveness really begins to look different from bitterness or punishment. It's easy to draw the line in the sand and say, "You crossed the line." It's much harder to say, "You've crossed the line, and I'm coming over there to bear the debt with you. Let's make our way back together." That's what forgiveness does. It doesn't erase the debt. It owns it.

Forgiveness Focuses on God's Power to Redirect a Situation

Joseph didn't try to punish his brothers for the evil they did. After Joseph established the debt of his brothers' evil, he simply said, "God meant it for good." He focused on God and trusted Him to do any sorting out that still needed to be done.

Debbie Morris did not willfully withhold her forgiveness to punish

Robert Willie. She gracefully extended it and allowed God and the government to do their part in his life.

You and I must not attempt to punish a spouse who has hurt us. That's not part of our job in the forgiveness process. That job belongs to God. Unfortunately, we girls often like to maintain control at this point.

We see this in action in *The Crucible*. Set in the town of Salem, Massachusetts, during the notorious witch trials, this play visualizes unforgiveness as the horrid hate that it is. It's not the witch-hunting I'm talking about, but a little side story that hits much closer to home.

John Putnam is found to have been in an adulterous affair. He humbly confesses to his wife, Elisabeth, and works every day to earn her forgiveness. He yearns to be redeemed. He is broken and repentant.

She returns his efforts with suspicion, prideful glances, words that stretch the truth of what happened into something more, and a daily search for opportunities to bring his sin up. Hers is the sin of keeping a house cold through unforgiveness.

Eventually, both John and Elisabeth are wrongfully accused of witchcraft. Both are arrested and face certain death if they don't confess their sin and give the names of other witches. Public ridicule, dirty dungeons, and separation from their children follow.

In the wee hours of the morning, John is brought to Elisabeth so that she can talk him into confessing his witchcraft lest he be hanged that day. He speaks of his love for her and his children, but he begs her to let him die in honor rather than live as a liar.

Soft tears begin to flow from the once cold, dry eyes of Elisabeth Putnam. Her heart breaks. The thick, black crust of unforgiveness is shattered.

The faithful love and integrity of an adulterer facing death has finally broken the callous heart of the unforgiving wife. She asks for his forgiveness, which he is quick to offer.

You could question whose sin was graver. As for me, I would choose hers. He not only repented and attempted every day to live righteously, but he was quick to model the forgiveness that he so desperately wanted. She, on the other hand, allowed the impurities of judgment, bitterness, reactive anger, hatred, and "getting even" to reign in her heart and was just not willing to forgive. She wanted to be the master of her husband's punishment. But punishment is not a part of forgiveness. Forgiveness decisively submits to God to do the correcting.

Forgiveness Does Erase the Emotional and Spiritual Aches Caused by the Debt

When we verbalize forgiveness to others and enact that by not punishing them ourselves but allowing them to pay their debt in their own time, it releases us from the emotional victimization that unforgiveness creates . . . and if they reconcile with you, it can release them too.

Do you want God to do a great work in your marriage? Then forgive your husband just as Christ forgave you.

You can't model that kind of forgiveness alone. This is when the familiar Philippians 4:13 comes into play. It says, "I can do all things through Christ who strengthens me" (NKJV). (Yes, even forgive your husband. Even model the great forgiving love of Christ.) But beware! Once again, if you claim that verse you had better know what you are saying.

The phrase "through Christ who strengthens me" originally was written like this **"en twi endunamounti me."**

Huh? My commentaries written by much brighter students of the gospel tell me two important things.

1. The word for "through" was really a word that literally meant "to pass through." In other words, the power comes as you live in union and identification with Christ. You are so closely connected to Him in Spirit that it is as if you have carved a hole in His heart and squeezed right through it. (Sounds quite possible knowing the love of my Savior!)

2. Let's see if you see it. Do you see a familiar word in that Greek phrase? Read it and circle any part of it that might seem familiar. (Hint: Remember the dynamite power of God's Word and prayer!) Do you see it? The "endunamounti"! There it is again, that power strapped together through prayer and the God-breathed Bible.

All that to say this: You can forgive your husband and you must. But you can't do it without the dynamite power of Christ. (I don't want to nag, but did you schedule an hour to be alone with Him today?)

When you do forgive, you might be surprised at how quickly God works. I was.

"A SUCCESSFUL MARRIAGE IS THE UNION BETWEEN TWO GREAT FORGIVERS." ▪
⟋ ANONYMOUS

I pulled onto Sycamore Drive and I whispered a prayer.

There he was.

He had a suitcase in his hand, and he was headed toward his own car when he saw my van.

He looked good. Very good. He'd obviously been spending a lot of time in our pool. His skin was tan. His nose was peeling. It reminded me of the first time I'd met him. My heart warmed, and I wanted to rush to him and fall into his arms.

Instead, the greeting was formal.

He helped me take my suitcases into the house. Since there wasn't a lot of conversation taking place, I decided to stay busy to avoid breaking down. I started to sort our dirty laundry into piles.

"I need to hit the road," Bob said as he watched me.

"OK," I said, really not having a clue what to say but thinking, That's it?! I drove eighteen hours to hear you say you needed to hit the road?! I waited, praying for the ability to be kind.

"Dannah," he pleaded. Oh, how wonderful it sounded to hear him say my name.

"Yeah?" I encouraged.

"In all these years, you've never once forgiven me for hurting you," he said.

"You've never asked," I told him, softening a little.

"I'm asking," he said. "Will you forgive me?"

"Oh, yes!" I affirmed.

Tears slipped down our cheeks as we fell into each other's arms and onto the laundry. And there in the dirty, smelly white pile, we held each other.

God was doing some washing of His own that day. And it felt glorious.

It's Your Turn

I'd like to encourage you to journal forgiveness to our husband—if you're truly willing to extend it. Write your list, and give it to God. ■

NOTE

1. Neil T. Anderson, *The Bondage Breaker* (Eugene, Oreg: Harvest House, 1996), 196.
2. Debbie Morris, *Forgiving the Dead Man Walking* (Grand Rapids: Zondervan, 2000).

"[God desires] that you may become

blameless and pure."

PHILIPPIANS 2:15

CHAPTER FOURTEEN

Cultivating the Purity of the Pearl

"I'm glad you guys are still married," whispered a pastor friend of ours as he passed us during the community craft fair.

The word was out.

It wouldn't have been easy to explain why Bob and I spent more than a month apart, and we never tried to make excuses. We just told the truth. People mistakenly assumed that we had been on the brink of divorce. They made comments that displayed a total lack of understanding.

"Divorce was never an option," I would always want to shout. "We did what we did to build our marriage, not to break it!"

What made it all the more difficult was that there was still a lot to work through. For each moment of blessed victory in our marriage, there seemed to be a night of crying to remind us how far we still had to go.

Our business fell apart as we abandoned it to focus on our faith and our marriage.

We chose to sell our precious little home to pay off debt. It felt more like we were losing it.

Eventually, we both left the corporate world that we were so impassioned to be in.

It seemed like there was always another challenge . . . another change . . . another sacrifice to protect this precious relationship.

I wondered if we'd ever arrive.

Do you ever get the feeling that your spiritual life is a roller coaster? That one week you are overwhelmed by your pathetic state of sin and the next you're on a mountaintop? I do. And I feel that way about my marriage sometimes. But there's actually good news in the midst of the pain.

The pearl is actually the result of a painful and difficult process. It is, in fact, an abnormal growth that occurs when a mollusk is invaded by a foreign particle such as a grain of sand. A diseased secretion would form if the pearl did not begin to produce calcium, which creates the nacre that makes the pearl look so pure and beautiful. After months or years of continually soothing and coating the point of pain, the world's only ready-to-wear gem is complete.

Just as the purity of the pearl is created out of adversity and impurities, so do our lives and our marriages become pure through a process. We can understand this process by embracing three basic truths.

You Were Not Born Pure

You were not born pure. Psalm 51:5 says, "Surely I was sinful at birth, sinful from the time my mother conceived me." How were you born? Sinful! You may have been innocent when you were born, and you can do plenty to rob yourself of some of that innocence, but you were not born pure. Just as the mollusk had within it the secretions to create disease, we have within us the seed of sin.

Your marriage was a union between two sinners . . . even though you may have been blinded by love for a few months or years.

Hopefully, both you and your husband have reached out to our great Savior for forgiveness of those sins. The moment we commit our lives to Christ and accept His precious blood as payment for our own sad, sinful nature, we begin the exciting journey toward becoming Christlike. Of course, that presents a few challenges of its own.

You Will Face Impurities

You *will* face impurities and temptation in your life. Your marriage will "feel" not so great sometimes as you face temptation individually or together. In Luke 17:1a, Jesus says, "Things that cause people to sin are bound to come." That's a promise I could do without. But the plain, simple fact is this: You and I can be sure we will face temptation. You will face monsters like anger, self-pity, greed, and lust.

The tough times will come. They did for Anne Graham Lotz. She writes:

Without my noticing it, the busyness had overtaken me, and I awoke one morning to the realization that I was in a marriage where the love had run out. I will never forget that panicked, trapped feeling as I knelt in prayer with tears streaming down my face, desperately pleading with the Lord for help . . . Was I condemned to live the rest of my life in a shell of a marriage relationship, keeping up a superficial front for our children, friends, family, and the general public, while my heart felt lifeless? Would I ever get used to the heaviness and pain? How could I endure? How could I live a life of hypocrisy? What would happen if I was ever found out? [1]

Of course, the Lord worked wonderfully in her marriage. But if Anne Graham Lotz can find such disappointment, can't you . . . can't I?

If you are like I used to be, when you meet that impurity, it will make you feel like you are starting *allllll* over again. But that is not entirely true. There's good news. Just look at the third powerful truth about your purity.

You Can Become Pure

You can *become* pure just like Philippians 2:15 says. God desires "that you may become blameless and pure." *You* can become pure. *Your marriage* can become pure.

In fact, meeting up with that impurity is an opportunity to develop purity. Just like that mollusk begins to cover that little invading grain of sand with nacre and make it beautiful, we have the opportunity to make right choices and turn our impurities into purity.

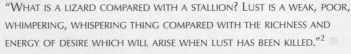

"WHAT IS A LIZARD COMPARED WITH A STALLION? LUST IS A WEAK, POOR, WHIMPERING, WHISPERING THING COMPARED WITH THE RICHNESS AND ENERGY OF DESIRE WHICH WILL ARISE WHEN LUST HAS BEEN KILLED." [2]

— C. S. LEWIS

C. S. Lewis shows us this when he spins a tale in *The Great Divorce*. He imagines ghostly people visiting heaven, and he writes about a slimy red lizard clinging to a certain ghost. The lizard taunted and teased that poor ghost, whispering great lies to him every day. (Sound like lust? gluttony? self-pity?) The ghost tried to control the lizard, rather than live without him.

An angel appeared and offered to rid the ghost of the little lizard. The ghost understood that to be relieved of the lizard it would be necessary to kill it. The ghost wasn't quite sure he could live without the lizard. After all, he'd known him for so long.

The rationalizations began. The ghost thought he might tame the lizard or release it gradually. The angel insisted the gradual approach would not work, as this red lizard was a very good liar. It was either the death of the lizard or the defeat of the ghost.

Finally, the ghost gave the angel permission to remove the lizard. The lizard screamed as it was twisted from the shoulder it clung to. With one great twist of the wrist, the angel sent it directly to the ground, where the impact broke its back. Then, an amazing thing happened. The ghost suddenly became a perfect man, and the limp, dead lizard was transformed into a very-much-alive silver and gold stallion. The new man leaped onto the great horse, and they rode off into the distance.

As Lewis explains, "What is a lizard compared with a stallion? Lust is a weak, poor, whimpering, whispering thing compared with the richness and energy of desire which will arise when lust has been killed."[3]

How do you become pure? By making right choices (or living righteously), even in the face of temptation like that evil dude Lust, you actually are afforded the great opportunity to develop purity. As you face the lust and make right choices to deny it and let Christ cover it with His great healing power, your impurities are transformed into the Christlike character of purity.

When I began to understand these three important truths, I suddenly realized that each time my marriage hit a rough period, it didn't mean we were starting all over again. We *may* get stuck in a period of discontent or even outright sin from time to time, but the totality of my experiencing meant I was moving on in God's grace to become pure.

Had you told me in the midst of our "time-out" that the coldness of my heart would be warmed by my husband's spiritual growth, I would have questioned your judgment of the situation. But when he turned back to God, a miraculous transformation took place. Slowly his hardness was replaced with comfortable touching. The hollowness of his presence was replaced with a direct gaze into my eyes. His contented apathy toward his faith turned into a fiery passion I could not compete with.

At one point, I wanted him to learn the discipline and blessing of a spiritual fast. I had little hope that he would participate in my plan to fast together for one day, but I gave it to God. I was soon writing this in my journal:

"24 days ago I pleaded with You to bring my dear husband to a new level of spirituality. I begged You not to let me come to You alone. Miracle of miracles! Two days later my husband began a fast that lasted 20 days. I saw Jesus in him and, as a result, I saw Jesus in this house."

(And by the way, I didn't ask him to fast. *He* asked me. Isn't God good?)

Purity and passion in my marriage is not the absence of pain and problems. There will be moments of sad defeat. It's all a part of the process. Those moments of pain may just be the things God uses to help us craft a beautiful, pure pearl out of this marriage.

Purity is a process. It is the process of making right choices that transform temptation into purity.

I was not born pure . . . and my marriage is not made up of two pure people.

We will face temptation, perhaps over and over again, but that in itself is not a sin. Rather, it is a chance to develop purity by talking to God and making right choices.

We can become pure.

Grasp that! It will save you a whole lot of confusion and "feelings" of defeat.

It's Your Turn

Using your journal, write about a time when you could see how God used a hurt in your marriage to bring you closer together. Praise God for that time. If you can't think of one, give God a current hurt and ask Him to begin to use it.

NOTES
1. Anne Graham Lotz, *Just Give Me Jesus* (Nashville: Word, 2000), 45.
2. C. S. Lewis, *The Great Divorce* (New York: Macmillan, 1946), 104.
3. ibid

CHAPTER FIFTEEN

Dreaming of the Pearl

"You coming in?" I asked Bob as the kids piled out of the van.

"Naw," he grumbled, seeming suddenly upset.

"What's wrong?" I prodded.

"Look at that house, Dannah," he said.

I knew what he meant. He didn't have to explain. A year and a half ago we'd sold our home to pay off debt, and we still weren't quite finished paying things off. Sometimes it hurt a little to be reminded.

I took the kids inside. They were joining my cousin's kids here to swim in the indoor pool. It was some house. Part of me wanted to succumb to the sick realization that our foolish greed had resulted in the loss of our own home, but I felt too stubborn to give in to that. After all, we were happier than ever. Our kids were happier than ever. I wouldn't have ever traded where we were for that little old house.

I came back out to the van with a twinkle in my eye.

"Let's go look at houses," I said.

"Dannah, we can't afford a house," Bob responded.

"Well, then let's just dream," I said. "You remember dreaming!"

He sat there reluctant for just a moment, and then a smile broke across his face.

"Then let's go look at really expensive ones!" he suggested.

We drove through neighborhoods with homes that cost $500,000 and up. We visited a builder's office and got land maps and picked out our little dream lot, which cost $99,000. As in $99,000 more than we had!

It was free and fun and perhaps the most wonderful afternoon we'd had in a long while.

on't ever stop dreaming. I hope that doesn't sound contradictory to all this caution against "stuff" and "status" I've been suggesting. You have to dream in a holy way.

Dreaming doesn't mean you become discontent with where you are. Do be careful. Philippians 4:11-12 tells us that Paul had learned to "be content whatever the circumstances. I know what it is to be in need, and I know what it is to have plenty. I have learned the secret of being content in any and every situation, whether well fed or hungry, whether living in plenty or in want."

And Paul knew what it was to be in a tough situation. Remember, he'd endured shipwrecks, being stuck on a deserted island, jail, and much more than you and I ever will. I think you and I can live with a tiny little rental house, a smaller paycheck than the Smiths, a title that doesn't sound as glamorous as the one you thought you'd have, and fewer toys than everyone else around you. It's really not that bad.

The exciting thing is that when you embrace where you are and you are content with it, unholy grasping gives way to really fun dreaming.

The day we felt led to sell our home to pay off debt, I cried. I loved that little house, but holding on to it meant clinging to our fake pearls of stuff and acquiring it through debt. The pearl of our marriage would become more beautiful as we relinquished all that stuff, but that would not occur without a lot of tears. I went to bed the night we realized we needed to sell telling the Lord that it would just be too hard on Robby and Lexi to lose their big yard, the pool with wraparound deck, and the grand sky fort. The next morning, God lovingly and boldly approached me. The first verse I read was Proverbs 14:26, which says, "He who fears the LORD has a secure fortress, and for his children it will be a refuge." (Yes, I wrote that down as an altar!)

I cried! I sat there on my deck realizing that God was asking me to obey and honor Him and trust Him to build a fortress mightier than this little home for me. I began to let go.

We priced our home higher than the real estate agent suggested during a time when homes were selling in nine to twelve months in our market. Our house sold in just a few weeks, and doors opened for us to move back to our hometown of Pennsylvania, where we found a little rental house.

At the end of one year, my cousin Jill was hanging out at our home while the kids played. She just happened to mention a little house that she'd seen listed today that was going to go fast. It was nice and she thought it was underpriced. It had an in-ground pool. By the end of the day, my parents had gone through it with us and wanted to help us get in. Jill prayed with us on the steps of that house and asked God to open the door if it was meant to be. We made a full-price cash offer. It was declined due to the seller's moral obligation to take an offer that came in just three hours before ours.

I cried. How many times would I have to give up this dream?

A few weeks later there was a sign in the yard across the street declaring the house "for sale by owner." It was soooo tiny. Tinier than the rental we were in. My husband wanted to buy it to get out of the rental trap.

I cried. Did God really want me to live in *that?*

The sellers decided the next day to list the house, and that took it out of our price range.

I told my pastor about "God's promise" to me that He "has a secure fortress" just waiting and that it will be a "refuge" for my kids. He told me that I already had the fortress. He told me that he believed God meant a spiritual and emotional fortress, pointing to where God has brought us since we gave up our home.

I cried. I didn't like that idea, but I believed it was from God.

Each time, I realized I couldn't dream about a home. I was still worshiping the idea of having a house. Focusing on it would not have been dreaming, but striving.

As I write this, another year has gone by. It was just a few weeks ago that my husband and I took that little dream home tour. We're in a better place financially and can afford a small house on our own. (Definitely not any of the ones we drove by that day.) Last week we toured a really magnificent Cape Cod. My cousin saw to it that we were the first ones in on this one.

The market here is a twenty-four-hour market again. We had to make the decision and stop others from viewing the house or endure a bidding war.

As I walked through with Mom, I said, "I never imagined living in a house as nice as the one I had before, let alone *this*. I love it." My heart was sold. Everyone else in my family loved the house too. But my dad and my husband felt like talking rationally about it. Even my mom was worried about where I'd put my office. They all agreed that we shouldn't buy so quickly. After four hours of discussing it, we didn't make an offer. The house sold *the next morning*.

I didn't cry! Ha! Sure, I'm still being a little stubborn about it because I was totally outvoted. And in all reality, I can't imagine us finding a house like that in our price range. But is it remotely possible that I've finally released this grasping? Nah! Probably not completely. I do have to be careful. But I'm finally to the point where I can dream about it.

- Not pray about it, pleading for God to give it to me like a spoiled brat

- Not strive for it by driving around and looking at every house whose owner plops a sign in the yard

- Not mourn the lack of a home, because I see how great it has been right here where we are

Now I am free to dream because I'm not being controlled by an unholy passion. And dreaming is so important. Remember, the merchant who found the pearl of great price didn't find it by accident. I imagine he had been dreaming about the day he'd find it.

I dream about how beautiful my marriage will be one day. Sometimes I dream about internal character and spiritual traits, but other times I just let loose on some fun stuff. I know it'll take a lifetime to achieve the internal dreams, but the mini-goals keep Bob and I connected on our way to the big dream.

Some of our mini-goals include owning a home someday soon. Since before we were married, we both dreamed of having a house where teenagers would want to hang out, feel loved, and have fun. That means we want a basement complete with a big TV and a Ping-Pong table. Since we're only a few years away from having our own teenagers, we're hoping to realize that one soon. We dream about trips we will take together. Right now we'd like to go to the Tanque Verde Dude Ranch in Arizona where they hand you your horse reins along with the keys to your bungalow. We think this would be a great time of family bonding, but we can't afford it yet so we're still dreaming.

Dreaming has to be monitored. I cling to Psalm 119:36–37 to monitor my dreaming. It says, "Turn my heart toward your statutes and not toward selfish gain. Turn my eyes away from worthless things; preserve my life according to your word." You might notice that I quoted part of that verse earlier in the book because I used it when I knew my eyes were focused on worthless things. Today I pray that verse when I feel I'm in a place where I might be distracted from loving God above all. I prayed it last week when I was at the Christian Booksellers Association's international convention signing books and enjoying the blessed gift of being able to make my living as an author . . . but dreadfully aware of the commercialism and pride that surrounded me and was in me. I pray it for us as we consider building a home and I don't want to be consumed by it. But I hope I don't ever stop dreaming. I think it's a great gift from God.

Dreaming connects us. And as long as we guard carefully against striving for these things instead of receiving them as gifts in God's time, they're a great part of the big dream . . . becoming a beautiful example of the Pearl of Great Price.

It's Your Turn

What dreams do you share with your husband? (Not unholy strivings, but dreams . . . you'll be OK if you get them and still OK if you don't!) ▪

The pearl is used in the Bible to denote purity and

preciousness. It's believed that the "pearly gates"

mentioned in Revelation 21:21 are a reference back

to Jesus' parable of the Pearl of Great Price. After

all, Christ's death is the gate by which we enter into

heaven. Only through His purity are we made holy

and clean to enter into the kingdom of God.

CHAPTER SIXTEEN

Treasuring the Pearl

I sat in *the midst of a rumpled pile of Christmas wrap torn to shreds as Robby and Lexi joyfully revisited each gift they'd unwrapped. Amidst their chattering and giggles, I'd missed one last box. Bob reached under the tree and handed it to me along with an envelope. I opened the envelope first.*

My dearest Dannah:

What a year it has been. Given any distance from our life, I have to look back in awe of what God has brought us through . . . and how much He has blessed us.

As for the pearl, the luster created by its constant brushes with pain is a visible reminder of what God can do with a single grain of sand. Just as the pearl's beauty grows in its difficult environment, your beauty in my eyes grows more profound each day.

That God would choose me to be "one" with you is

beyond what I ever asked Him for.

    You are the pearl of my life, the poetry of my heart, the music of my spirit, and the blessing of each new morning.

—B

    She is mine own, And I as rich in having such a jewel
As twenty seas, if all their sand were pearl,
The water nectar, and the rocks pure gold.

*—S*HAKESPEARE

With tears in my eyes I opened the box to find a single big, beautiful pearl on a dainty gold chain. My husband kissed my nose and helped me put it on.

And there in our rental house where the wallpaper is fading and peeling off the walls, the place where I've come to know the Sears repair man by name because an appliance breaks every week, and where the yard outside is more weed than grass, and where the bills just barely get paid . . .

I stopped to ponder the treasure.

I sure didn't think it would look like this, but I'm so glad it does. The blessings God had for me were so much bigger than houses and careers and Jet Skis. I couldn't find what I was looking for in those things or even in the midst of them. I'm so glad God ripped my dreams out from under me. It's been a massive downpouring of blessings.

The biggest blessing is a marriage that's been humbled and through the pain has learned to seek to exemplify what it was created to portray . . . a passionate love between Christ and His bride, the church. We've got a long, long way to go, but the lessons of the pearl give us courage and keep us headed in the right direction. There are a few things I try to keep in mind:

I HAVE TO REMEMBER that *the pearl is not found accidentally, but as a result of an intentional pursuit.* It takes hard work to find the treasure in my marriage. I'm determined to keep finding it. With each layer of digging I find the treasure to be purer and more precious.

I HAVE TO REMEMBER that *the pearl is of great value and costs us everything*. If I lost "it all" tomorrow and had just my husband and my children, I'd be OK. The rest is just stuff. I've learned that by losing it. I'm still standing.

I HAVE TO REMEMBER that *the impurities within our marriage are actually great opportunities to cultivate a precious gem.* This week has been hard for us. I sure don't feel like finishing a book that outlines our moments of shame and shares the great victories. What we're facing seems piddly compared to some monsters we've beaten, but we are a tad disappointed, not in each other but in us, this week. Ah, but the beautiful past and great healing—as well as the many joyful second honeymoons —give me hope for the future in spite of the obstacles we face. This pain too will be a part of the beauty of our marriage.

MOSTLY I HAVE TO REMEMBER that *if I want my marriage to fulfill its purpose of reflecting the relationship of Christ and His church, I have to stay close to the Pearl of Great Price* so I can recognize the impurities and the path to victory.

Mrs. Billy Graham was once at a grand dinner party in London, England, where she was seated next to the former head of Scotland Yard. She was enthralled by his career and asked him to tell more about it. She was particularly curious about his work in exposing forgery and counterfeiting. When she suggested to him that he'd probably spent a lot of time studying counterfeit signatures, he corrected her, "On the contrary, Mrs. Graham, I spent all of my time studying the genuine thing. That way, when I saw a counterfeit I could immediately detect it."

Oh, my friend, stay close to Jesus. Stay closer than you think is possible. Study His love so you'll immediately detect the counterfeits that tempt you. Experience His love so you can reflect it for the world to see in a truly "mysterious" love-life with your husband.

*M*AY OUR MARRIAGE AND YOURS

BE A PORTRAIT OF OUR DEVOTION

TO THE PEARL OF GREAT PRICE.

HE COSTS EVERYTHING.

HE IS WORTH THE COST.

APPENDIX A

APPENDIX A

LOVE NOTES FROM CHRISTIAN CELEBRITIES

An Interview with Stormie Omartian

Best-selling author of *The Power of a Praying Wife*

I had the thrill of meeting Stormie at the Christian Booksellers Convention. When she gracefully arrived in the hospitality suite reserved by her publisher, all heads turned. Hers did not. She is a beautiful woman, but she doesn't seem to take note of it herself.

As we sat there with the crowd buzzing around us, she gave me her complete, selfless attention and even let me peek into some of the most intimate moments of her marriage to Christian musical mastermind Michael Omartian. Listen to the candid, loving testimony of a woman who has taught hundreds of thousands of women to pray for their husbands!

DANNAH: *One of the challenges you issue in your book* The Power of a Praying Wife *is to replace nagging with prayer. That's a really hard one, especially if there is impurity or betrayal on the part of the husband. What's the difference between nagging and godly confrontation?*

STORMIE: *Are you talking about an affair or betrayal?*

DANNAH: *It may even be flirting or pornography. It doesn't have to be an outright affair.*

STORMIE: Yes. I've known too many Christian artists who flirted and thought it was OK and it ended up destroying their marriage. That can be very destructive. It's the beginning. Things can creep in. You have to be so cautious. Temptation is around us all the time. To pretend that it isn't is to be in denial or in a dream world.

I never want a woman to feel like she can't share her needs or her thoughts. I don't want her to think she has to be a doormat in any way. She should confront her husband.

To not do that, you are living with a lie. The thing is, the nagging is when you keep saying the same thing over and over. You have to lay it all out there for him. Tell him this behavior is unacceptable and that you are not willing to live with it and that you want to get help together.

DANNAH: And you really have to go to God before you go to your husband, right?

STORMIE: Yes! It's only been once or twice in our marriage when I sensed another woman moving in. Women sense that. The men sometimes don't. But I'd always just go to the Lord and say, "Lord, this is something unholy." It wasn't that I didn't trust my husband, because I do. One of the things I respect about him most is that he is very loyal. It is his greatest quality in my mind . . . his faithfulness. But I just sensed something from the other woman and I prayed, "Lord if there are unholy intentions in this woman's life or in her mind, take her out of my husband's life." The Lord answered that prayer swiftly. She'd be transferred or she would move away or something.

DANNAH: There wasn't the need to act out in jealousy?

STORMIE: No! I don't even think he was aware of it. He didn't see anything. But women sense these things. In the couple instances where I sensed that, I prayed for the Lord to remove the problem and He did. When we act out in jealously or anger, we look like small, pitiful women. How much more effective when we go to the Lord and say, "If I'm off in this, show me." There was one time early in our marriage when a young woman came into our lives who was a threat to me because she was so amazingly attractive. I couldn't imagine that Michael wouldn't be attracted to her. But God straightened me out. I prayed about it and He gave me peace, because there was nothing to worry about from either of them.

DANNAH: What advice do you give to women who are isolating themselves during those times when we feel jealous or know of an actual threat to our marriage?

STORMIE: I think it is so important to have someone who's ahead of you. I was a mentor for a younger woman. She was jealous of her boyfriend's former girlfriend even though the former girlfriend had never been anything significant to him. "The jealousy," I told her, "is going to be your downfall. Because if you let that seed grow, it will be like a cancer. It will erect a wall between you. It will tear you apart. You've got to take it to the Lord." She said it really helped her because she was able to let it go by just talking it through it and praying about it.

DANNAH: Let's change focus here. Give us Stormie's Secret Tip to keeping your husband attracted.

STORMIE: I always try to take care of my body and my appearance. I always work at staying attractive to him and to myself. I don't let myself get too overweight or too exhausted or too sick. I ask myself, When he leaves the house, what is he remembering? When he is at work and the women are all put together, will he remember the old, overweight housewife back home with gray roots, or will he remember an attractive wife? *I work at it.*

When I started praying for my husband, God really revealed a lot to me about men. For example, God showed me that He put into man this need for sex. *Woman have a need for closeness, and sex can be a part of it. But men have a total physical need for sex. If we are denying them that because we are mad at them or whatever . . . if we are denying them that release, we are suffocating that need that God created in them. I urge women to make themselves attractive so you feel attractive. Then, make that effort to meet his need.*

DANNAH: Do you think the sexual relationship has a special ability to bring intimacy between two spouses who love God?

STORMIE: Yes, it brings down the walls. The devil is always trying get a wedge between you. Always. There is such power when a man and woman are in unity physically. When the devil tries to break that down, don't let him.

DANNAH: Give us a snapshot of your marriage. Tell us something very specific that happened in your life. Show us a moment when you can say, "I am proud of my decision to protect the purity of my marriage."

STORMIE: *There was a time when I was going through a really hard struggle in my marriage. You know, one of those times when everything is dying. You just feel hopeless. You aren't communicating well. Then, into our lives comes this man that my husband is working with, and I feel a sudden strong attraction to him. I was so shocked. It was really strong. I thought, Oh, I am going to grieve the Holy Spirit. Now, the man never knew I felt this, but I was so concerned about it. I was upset that it was even in me. I went that afternoon into my prayer closet and laid on the floor on my face and cried and fasted and prayed and said, "God I am not leaving here until this is broken." I had to continue it through the next day because it was so strong. The feeling was gut-wrenching as I stayed there with my face in the carpet and kept praying, "I can do all things through Christ who strengthens me."*

God broke it completely. It was so totally gone that when I looked at that person the next time I thought, What was that all about! I was not attracted to him at all. It was a setup by the devil because my marriage was struggling.

DANNAH: *I've struggled with that once, too. I think most women do, but we don't talk about it.*

STORMIE: *Yes, it's very common. We've just got to talk about it and say, "This can happen, and it is wrong." We cannot allow ourselves to become attracted to people of the opposite sex. The minute that feeling hits you, you should be on your face and asking God to break it. It is so of the devil.*

DANNAH'S PICK OF STORMIE'S BOOKS:

If you haven't read *The Power of a Praying Wife*, you must! It has taught hundreds of thousands of women to pray powerfully for their husbands. It is a must-have for your library.

An Interview with Lisa Ryan

Co-host of CBN's *700 Club*

Lisa Ryan and I talked by telephone one sunny spring day. She wasn't easy to catch up with as we had to reschedule a few times so she could . . . finish her first book, attend her daughter's special school event, and cut some voice-overs for the 700 Club. (And I'm betting she was probably at Taco Bell with her husband, Marcus, in between all of that . . . read on to see what I'm talking about!) Here's a woman who seems to "have it all" but has some godly wisdom against striving for that.

DANNAH: Lisa, you've just come off of a busy year as you've finished your first book. Tell me about it.

LISA: For Such a Time as This *is in response to the many challenges facing young women in this generation. It looks at the life of Esther—a countercultural girl. The messages are timeless, and it can apply to any woman at any point in her life, but this is really for women who would be Esther's peers.*

She is an example for them today . . . a model from the Word of God. The character at work in her life positions her to become a woman of destiny. She would not have been plucked out to be a woman of destiny had the character not been in her life already. The choices she made positioned her to be ready. There is a call in there for the reader to rise up and be a woman of destiny like Esther. God is calling out modern-day Esthers in this generation . . . for such a time as this.

DANNAH: You are a woman of destiny. The position you are in is much like Esther's as you influence so many. Did you have to make choices . . . tough choices . . . to build character before you were called to that position?

LISA: After having been Miss California and as a young married woman with no children—I was really pursuing a TV career in California. I was just beginning to get some significant roles and opportunities. During that time, I got pregnant with our first child, but continued pursuing that whole career thing. A year into dragging our daughter off to auditions with me, I realized, "I'm a mother now. That has to be my priority now. I can't do it all now."

DANNAH: What did you do as a result of realizing that?

LISA: I walked away from the career completely, but that dream died a slow, painful death.

DANNAH: Did that hurt?

LISA: It did hurt. In my ignorance and immaturity, I thought, That's it! My life's over. God's never gonna use me again. *I'm embarrassed to admit that as a daughter of the feminist movement, I didn't value motherhood. I was disappointed feeling like maybe I hadn't done all that I should have done career-wise before I entered this season of my life. I felt like a TV career wasn't meant to be anymore.*

DANNAH: You let go of the dream?

LISA: Yeah, I put it on the shelf like an unfinished book and told God if it ever came down He would have to do that. I threw myself into motherhood and my marriage.

DANNAH: What differences did you see in your marriage and family?

LISA: I used to think I would find contentment "doing it all" and "being it all." I thought it would come in all of the professional accomplishments that would bring recognition . . . the trophy things. To my surprise, I was most content when I let go of those things. I embraced where I was at the moment . . . I didn't know the future and I stopped striving. I was much more at peace as a person, as a woman when I finally rested in it. I finally found the contentedness that I was always looking for.

DANNAH: You are certainly in the TV business now . . . in a position of favor. Did that happen right away after you laid it down?

LISA: No! There were several very difficult years in between as my husband and I walked through a devastating financial setback. Ultimately we came to

Virginia for my husband to get a graduate degree. He was a businessman, and we were involved in ministry. At the time we had two children and one on the way. We knew it would be a sacrifice for us to move across the country and go to grad school, but we didn't know how much. It took everything financially to get here and sustain us. We thought surely we could find a townhouse or something we could afford, but we couldn't. God said no. This was an investment time. We sacrificed and lived in student housing (which at the time was further humbling). It turned out to be such a blessing.

My husband was diving into studies, and I had our third daughter right after we landed here. Soon, there was a job that opened up at CBN in operations. Operations is the team that runs the cameras, TelePrompTer—all the behind-the-scenes stuff. I really did not want to go back to work because I had the baby. I had finally found a contentedness in being a stay-at-home mom.

Marcus and I discussed it. It would be a reversal of roles for a season. So, I went to work and he became "Mr. Mom."

DANNAH: How did it come about that you became a co-host?

LISA: It was a total God thing. Several months after I'd been here at CBN, it came to someone's attention that I had worked in television before and had even done some work for CBN in years past. I'd given my testimony as Miss California as well as guest-hosted the 700 Club a couple of times. Now here I was in my jeans and a ponytail behind the scenes and God began to orchestrate. It was a Cinderella story, really, how the Lord just plucked me out of that behind-the-scenes position. I came to the attention of Pat Robertson. You might say he discovered me. Someone asked if I'd be willing to do a camera test. I was a little hesitant. I just wanted to make sure it was God and not me.

DANNAH: So you waited rather than pursued it?

LISA: The Lord opened the opportunity for me to work on camera. It was so much more redeeming than what I was doing in California. Only the Lord knew that working for the 700 Club had been a hidden desire in my heart for many years.

DANNAH: The things you were doing when you were working so hard for it before you gave it all up and obeyed God by staying at home for a season?

LISA: *I was* knocking myself out *before. And now God just brought it about in such an easy way. There was just no striving in it.*

DANNAH: *Do you think that would have happened if you hadn't made some sacrifices to let go of the dream?*

LISA: *One of the things I discovered in writing about Esther is that obedience is the seed that's planted that brings God's favor on your life. Perhaps it was obedience at a certain point in my life—giving up the dream of a TV career—that brought God's favor to my life at this point. Right before I gave up the career search, I had done a TV interview with Lee Ezell, who is an author and notable conference speaker. I asked her, "Can a Christian woman have it all?" She said, "Sure, a Christian woman can have it all; she just can't have it all at the same time." That helped me. There are times and seasons for us as Christian women. You have to be true to the season that you are in.*

DANNAH: *That's a revolutionary idea in a day and age when we're told we should have it all.*

LISA: *It is. We are the daughters of the feminist movement. We have been told that a woman has to do it all to be a successful woman. Successful career . . . successful marriage . . . successful kids . . . looking sharp. That's what the feminist movement pitched. As Christian women, we took that ideology on and just applied it to ministry. Somewhere along the line we forgot the discipline of saying no.*

DANNAH: *Is the discipline of saying no a matter of protecting your marriage?*

LISA: *Well, let me backtrack a little. We really do, as Christian women, look at the "big" impurities as pornography and adultery and we say, "Oh, Lord, I never want to let that into my life." But it's the little impurities that we give way to in our marriage that set us up for those bigger things. So many times we are not aware of those little things, you know, "the little foxes that spoil the vine" (Song of Songs 2:15). I am preaching to myself when I say I think we are too busy. I have to stop myself and say that my marriage and my family have got to come first—before a job, before a book, before a speaking engagement. If as a mom and a wife I am totally stressed out using my talents for God that I can't relax with my family . . . then I am not honoring God. Maybe the pastor or school teachers or Sunday school coordinators won't want me to give this advice, but sometimes we have to say no.*

    DANNAH: *You can't do it all!*

    LISA: *Of course, I want to bake cupcakes for my kid's class, or go after that next great interview for my job . . . but sometimes we can only do so much and that needs to be OK. You can't take on every ministry at church. You might be one of a small handful of people that get things done, but you still need to say no sometimes. If your husband is the last thing on your "to-do" list rather than the first person on your "want-to-do list," he is going to know that . . . he will sense that. He'll know he is getting the crumbs off the table. We must consciously make ourselves aware of when we are getting so busy that he is becoming one of the last things on our list.*

    DANNAH: *What's one way that busyness affects marriages?*

    LISA: *Exhaustion is the number one killer of libido for women. If you are exhausted from what you are doing for everyone else, you are not honoring the covenant you have made not only with your husband but with God. I think too many times we are willing to sacrifice the covenant with our spouse for little things. If I do that, I am breaching my covenant with God. That wakes me up a little bit to think of it like that. I need to have the energy to give him my mind, my emotions, and my intimacy. It is a sin to give my best to everyone and everything else.*

    DANNAH: *How do you do that in your marriage?*

    LISA: *Our kids are ten, seven, and five, so we are very busy. We have to make a conscious effort to make each other our best friend. I have girlfriends. He has guy friends. But we spend most of our free time with each other as opposed to those friends or doing individual recreation activities.*

    People laugh at us here at CBN. Some of the single girls come to me and note that Marcus and I go out to lunch together three or four times a week. They say things like, "Whenever we see you in the car you are talking, talking, talking." We tell each other everything that's going on in our individual lives . . . activities, feelings, people, everything.

Our favorite thing to do is to run to Taco Bell! We might have just thirty minutes together there. We just stay in constant communication. It's time invested in making us each other's best friend.

DANNAH: *What's your number one word of advice to married women?*

LISA: *Number one word of advice? Read Stormie Omartian's* The Power of a Praying Wife. *Be your husband's intercessor and do warfare for him. No one can pray for him with knowledge like you can, not even his mother. Before I ever read her book, that principle was critical in my marriage. A close second is, be cautious about how you speak about your husband to other people. Even if you are going through a difficult time . . . don't wear that to the world. As a young bride, I foolishly made the mistake of talking too much and hurt my husband deeply. He felt so betrayed. Honor and guard your husband's reputation. I'm not saying you should bottle it up. Find that* one *Christian woman who is older and wiser and who can guide you through spiritually, but be very careful how you speak about your husband to everyone else. The Enemy will take that. He will use just one little thing. If another man hears you saying something disparagingly about your husband, the Enemy could use that. Women are drawn away through conversation. Eve was drawn away by the serpent through conversation. Women are still drawn away by conversation. Guard your marriage by the way you talk about your husband and the conversations you have with other men. God has brought my husband and I through so much. I am grateful for the people who were there to give me good advice in the early years of my marriage.* ■

DANNAH'S PICK OF LISA RYAN'S BOOKS:
For Such a Time as This by Lisa Ryan is a great release by Multnomah. You can see a taste of it in this interview. I don't know about you, but it makes me hungry for more!

Interview with Gary Chapman

Best-selling author of *The Five Love Languages*

My husband and I were honored to be seated with Gary and Karolyn Chapman at a Moody Press authors' appreciation dinner. What a living example of a happy marriage. They exude love . . . not just for each other but for everyone they meet. They'll be the first to tell you that it hasn't been easy. For that very reason, they've been able to minister to many as they boldly attempt to build strong marriages. The Five Love Languages *is Gary's best-selling book that has transformed thousands of marriages. The book teaches couples to recognize how their spouse communicates and receives love. It's very powerful. I highly recommend it. Bob and I were energized by their example. I was able to grab Gary for a few minutes and ask him a few questions about his marriage.*

DANNAH: *Is it ever possible to love someone you hate? You pose that question in your book* The Five Love Languages. *Is it possible?*

GARY: *It depends on what your definition of love is. Hate is a deep, deep emotion that comes at the end of hurt and anger and bitterness. It is a strong emotion that really is against the person and wishes them ill. It is difficult to have positive feelings toward a spouse when you hate them. But in the Bible love is not based on a feeling. It's based on thinking and a way of behaving. It is the attitude that says, "I choose to look out for your best interest." In that sense, yes! It is possible to hate your husband and love him at the same time. Love chooses to do something positive for him in spite of the hurt and anger and bitterness. When you choose that, you have a positive impact on the climate of the marriage.*

DANNAH: *To see somebody model it is what gives us courage to do it, so in your own marriage give us an example. Maybe the emotion was not as strong as hatred. It could be just discomfort. Is there a moment that your wife chose to enact that concept, and it influenced the way you responded to her?*

GARY: *In the early years of our marriage, we had tremendous struggles in our marriage. We went through six, seven years of struggles. And really, both of us lost* our love feelings. If you had said then, "Do you have warm feelings for your wife?" I'd say, "No, I feel hurt." Basically because she wouldn't listen to me! [He laughs a little here as if to say, "OK, maybe it wasn't all her!" It was a process. Both of us came to the conclusion that we had to do something different. We went against the negative feelings and began to think in terms of the life of Jesus and His life of servanthood to other people. So, I'd start to think positively in spite of my lack of feelings; I'd look for ways to serve her. She began to reach out and do things for me. It turned our feelings around. It was the big turning point.

Since then, there are times when smaller things irritate us and create negative feelings. Every time I as a husband fail to do something she expected, negative feelings are stimulated in her. It is easy to have negative feelings toward your spouse. All it requires is that your spouse be human! They will disappoint you.

DANNAH: *Is there ever a time when a monitored separation is healthy?*

GARY: *I think it can be. Especially in cases where there is physical abuse or extreme verbal abuse or alcoholism or drug abuse. In those situations if something is not done to stop that pattern, the marriage is not going to survive. So as an act of love the wife says to the husband, "I love you too much to sit here and let you destroy me and yourself, and, consequently, the next time you come home drunk . . . or the next time you hit me . . . I will walk out the door and be gone for three days." I think a temporary separation can be healthy. I think a wife in that situation needs to have a place she can go. She needs to be ready to do that.*

But if it is going to be love it has to be seen as that. It is not abandonment. The motivation is "I want to be an agent of love." I also think that if that happens and she leaves for three days, then the next time it needs to be longer. Eventually, she will stay away until he gets help and his counselor assures her there is healing.

Again, it's not divorce. It's not even thinking divorce. It's motivated by love. This should come after a person has tried soft love over a period of time. There should be a genuine attempt at soft love before tough love ever enters the picture.

DANNAH: *What do you do when one spouse is completely unwilling to participate in the healing process? Maybe he won't go to counseling or won't even acknowledge that there is a problem.*

GARY: *I deal with that pretty thoroughly in* Loving Solutions. *It's for a person . . . who is married to an alcoholic, or is depressed, or who will not be sexually involved with you . . . tough things. Sometimes you think you have two options. "Either stay in the marriage and be miserable all of my life. Or get out of the* marriage." What I'm trying to say in that book is that there is a third alternative. You can see yourself as a change agent. You can do a little homework to find out how you will be a change agent. Even though your spouse will not go to counseling, they will change for better or for worse. The question is, "How can I have a positive influence on that?" In most cases, the wife is doing what will have a negative influence because she does what comes naturally. There are things a wife can do to make the change positive. For example, a wife engaging the husband in a conversation about his childhood. Just asking questions and asking about his relationship with his father, brothers, and mother. She may well discover things about him that give her insight into his behavior. She can learn how to address some of the needs behind his behavior. You don't focus on changing the behavior; you focus on the need. Don't treat the symptom; treat the problem.

DANNAH: That's really hard to do when the anger is present?

GARY: Without God it's impossible. You don't deny your emotion; you acknowledge it, but you are also saying to God, "Lord, I want to be a loving agent in this marriage. I want to know how to love an unlovely husband." God's an expert in that because He loves us and we're unlovely sometimes. You choose to let God love him through you. If you can tap into that and begin to meet his needs, a high percentage of husbands will respond when a wife is reaching out with unconditional love.

DANNAH: Maybe a husband has had an affair or has ignored his wife sexually or is consumed by pornography—what impact can the love languages have on a situation like that? Have you ever seen the use of love languages have an impact on relationships where infidelity was a factor?

GARY: Learning to speak a spouse's love language will not automatically remove the hurt of infidelity. It takes time and it's not a quick fix, but learning to speak a spouse's love language and speaking it in spite of your hurt does create a climate that makes it possible for healing to take place. If we don't speak each other's love languages, we have empty love tanks. It's very difficult to heal on an empty love tank. If we start using the love languages, we create a positive emotional climate and can talk about our hurts. The love languages speed the healing process.

I've seen scores of couples work through infidelity. It can be done.

DANNAH: Is there a time when your wife used the love languages to defuse a difficult situation?

GARY: This was not a "difficult situation," but just this morning she used the love languages. I was about to leave the hotel room and she said, "Come back in here." I did and she smiled and said, "You look great!" I mean, you know, I walk out feeling like a million dollars. She was speaking my love language. She was saying, "I love you!"

When she gives me positive words, my love tank fills up and I feel warm toward her. I am ready to do anything for her. When I speak her love language, which is acts of service, the climate stays positive so that when I do have a disappointment, the love language minimizes the disappointed feelings.

Oh, I did think of something. We were on the way to the airport Sunday. I had gone to church and went home to pick her up, and she was all packed and ready to go. On the way to the airport I realized that the gas tank was empty. There wasn't enough gas to get to the airport. We were on a tight schedule, so I said to her, "I meant to do that earlier this morning, but I forgot. We don't have an option. We have to stop." She didn't come down on me with negative words. In our earlier years she would have. Instead she said, "We've got time." It made it easier. I knew I was wrong. I knew I hadn't lived up to her expectations. I hadn't lived up to my expectations.

DANNAH: That's got to feel really safe.

GARY: Yeah. I know she is going to look for the positive. She may be disappointed, but she has learned that saying something negative creates a negative atmosphere. The gas tank has to be filled no matter what. Why not have a positive climate while we do it!

DANNAH'S PICK OF GARY CHAPMAN'S BOOKS:

Definitely get The Five Love Languages *and go through it with your husband. My husband loves it. Better yet, he uses it to love me!*

Appendix B

The Pursuit of the Pearl Prayer Club for Women

Introduction

You are not alone in your desire to have a consuming, intimate relationship with your husband. Join the club! The club appendix study guide makes this book into a fun, interactive accountability group. So grab a few friends and read along together.

What Is It?

Each week you will read a chapter independently and do the journaling and prayer alone. Then, you'll come to your club time and discuss things a bit more deeply. Each week you will encourage one another to pursue a pure and fulfilling marriage union.

First you talk. You simply share the "It's Your Turn" part of each chapter. You may read your journaling assignment, which I highly recommend. Or you may simply summarize key thoughts. Then encourage each other as God leads you. It's easy and it's fun as you discuss ideas to make your marriages more fulfilling, encourage each other, and hold each other accountable.

Then you pray. At least thirty minutes of each Club session should be spent praying God's Word into your marriages. As you get deeper into the book, this becomes easier and more structured. At first, just pray as God leads you. But pray diligently.

We're In! How Can We Make It More Fun?

If you want to add a fun twist to the club, do it the way I do. Each club member brings one inexpensive pampering item. A packet of tea bags, a bar of scented soap, a votive candle, a new fingernail file, or a trial-sized hand lotion are some good ideas. At the beginning of club time, everyone places her item in a basket or in the center of the table. At the end of club time, everyone privately writes the name of one of the ladies on the paper. The lady you choose is one who has kept a tough commitment to love her husband in a specific way that week or who has done some extra research on the subject and shared ideas with you, or who has contributed in some special way. The woman with the most names for the week gets to take the armload of pampering gifts home. For example, one woman was struggling with how her husband ignored her during Monday Night Football. Her friends encouraged her to give him that time for himself and to be a part of it by making it special. She came back the next week reporting that instead of nagging, she made him a huge basketful of his favorite snacks and drinks and included a love note. He was crazy about it and it changed the direction of their whole week. She "won" the pampering basket for the week.

Who Leads It?

Hey, the good news is there is little to no preparation time. You just come to talk and fellowship. So anyone can lead it, or you can even take turns from week to week. Grab some friends and dive in! You'll have a lot of fun and find some real encouragement and accountability.

ACKNOWLEDGMENTS

THE PEOPLE IN THE STORY BEHIND THIS STORY

*U*nlike my first book, which recounted youthful mistakes that I'd hoped never to tell anyone, I approached this one with enthusiasm and confidence. My first book, *And the Bride Wore White*, had touched a tender nerve within the moms and adult youth leaders who read it. They were finding the healing they'd been looking for for years. I wanted to tell them the rest of the story. I was excited! But *now,* the book is on paper and my knees are knocking. The truth is sometimes great fodder for church gossip, and there's a lot of raw truth in this book. I am grateful to the people God used to move me forward as I came to realize how risky this work is.

Perhaps my first encouragement came from women who invested into my marriage and my life years before there was ever a book to be written. **Ramona Taylor** and **Elizabeth Duncan** cried with me, prayed with me, kept my feet on the ground when it was "not my fault" and lifted me up when I didn't think we'd make it. My life is ever reflective of their mentoring.

My mom and dad, **Dan** and **Kay Barker**, continue to encourage me because they fell in love and choose to stay in love. Thank you for the treasure.

My next dose of encouragement came from three people you know as well as I do. **Stormie Omartian** generously let me interview her and peek into her own marriage trials and triumphs. What a humble woman is packaged in that stunning beauty! **Gary Chapman** also obliged my request for some of his time for an interview and even read this *whole* manuscript for me—these books aren't so pretty when they're Word documents—and agreed to place his precious name on an endorsement. His joyful marriage with Karolyn is a powerful motivation to all who meet them. **Lisa Ryan**, my third "celebrity" featured in the book, was truly used of God's Spirit. My interview with her was delayed for several reasons and came just as I was beginning to realize how vulnerable I might look in this piece. But that day on the phone, it was as if God had scripted the words she said to confirm the direction of this book. She introduced me to Solomon's "little foxes" whom I'd met many times in my marriage, but I just didn't know they had been named. I'm so grateful to all three of these wonderful servants of God for giving to me and to you through this book.

But the most powerful encouragement came from **women I can't name**. You may know some of them, but they are still in the heat of the battle. I finished this work just prior to going to a gathering of thousands of Christians. Releasing it to my editor was frightening. God knew. That week at the gathering, two women deeply involved in Christian ministry tearfully recounted their pain caused by their husbands' addictions to pornography. "Don't back away from this cowardly bully," I felt God saying. Several weeks after returning from the gathering, and discussing with advisers and editors the controversial issue of confessing sexual sin, the phone calls came pouring in from women I'd never met but who'd heard me recount my confession of premarital sexual sin to my husband. These were women who were locked in a prison because they held a dark secret. They wanted out. "You found the way. Now light the way," it seemed as though God was saying. I'm grateful to the many who've called at just the right moment with just the right words to keep me courageous.

I'm grateful for Moody Press and those there who keep the right things prioritized. **Greg Thornton** and **Bill Thrasher** have continued to put up with Bob and me as we continue in our zealous approach to the publishing industry. **Elsa Mazon** and **Cheryl Dunlop** gave fantastic insight and helped me think through the delicacies of this book. **Dave DeWit** and **Julia Ryan** have created another masterpiece in their presentation of this message.

My final word of thanks goes to the friends I have now and those I'll have in the future who read this and love us still. Our marriage is a work in progress. Our sins can be recorded here in confidence that we've been rescued from them by the blood of Jesus. We want others to experience that too.

In Gratitude for What Christ Has Done

~Dannah